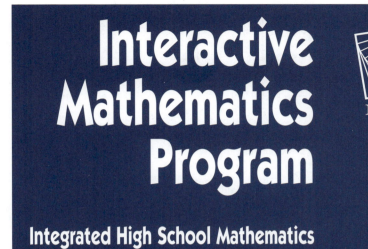

Interactive Mathematics Program

I M P

Integrated High School Mathematics

Y E A R **1**

The Pit and the Pendulum

Dan Fendel and Diane Resek
with
Lynne Alper and Sherry Fraser

KEY CURRICULUM PRESS
Innovators in Mathematics Education

This material is based upon work supported by the National Science Foundation under award number ESI-9255262. Any opinions, findings, and conclusions or recommendations expressed in this publication are those of the authors and do not necessarily reflect the views of the National Science Foundation.

™ Interactive Mathematics Program, IMP, and the IMP logo are trademarks of Key Curriculum Press.

Key Curriculum Press
P.O. Box 2304
Berkeley, California 94702
editorial@keypress.com
http://www.keypress.com

10 9 8 7 6 5 4 3   00 99 98 97
ISBN 1-55953-254-8
Printed in the
United States of America

Project Editor
Casey FitzSimons

Additional Editorial Development
Dan Bennett, Bill Finzer, Crystal Mills

Editorial Production
Caroline Ayres, Debbie Cogan,
Greer Lleuad, Jason Luz

Editorial Assistants
Jeff Gammon, Romy Snyder

Teacher Reviews
Dave Calhoun, John Chart, Dwight Fuller,
Donna Gaarder, Dan Johnson, Jean Klanica,
Cathie Thompson

Multicultural Reviews
Edward Castillo, Ph.D., Sonoma State University
Genevieve Lau, Ph.D., Skyline College

Cover and Interior Design
Terry Lockman
Lumina Designworks

Cover Photography and Cover Illustration
Hillary Turner and Tom Fowler

Production
Luis Shein

Production Coordination
Susan Parini

Technical Graphics
Greg Reeves

Illustration
Tom Fowler, Evangelia Philippidis,
Diane Varner, Martha Weston,
April Goodman Willy

Publisher
Steven Rasmussen

Editorial Director
John Bergez

Acknowledgments

Many people have contributed to the development of the IMP curriculum, including the hundreds of teachers and many thousands of students who used preliminary versions of the materials. Of course, there is no way to thank all of them individually, but the IMP directors want to give some special acknowledgments.

We want to give extraordinary thanks to the following people who played unique roles in the development of the curriculum.

- **Bill Finzer** was one of the original directors of IMP before going on to different pastures. He helped shape the overall vision of the program, and worked on drafts of several Year 1 units.

- **Matt Bremer** did the initial revision of every unit after its pilot testing. Each unit of the curriculum also underwent extensive focus group reexamination after being taught for several years, and Matt did the rewrite of many units following the focus groups. He has read every word of everyone else's revisions as well, and has contributed tremendous insight through his understanding of high school students and the high school classroom.

- **Mary Jo Cittadino** became a high school student once again during the piloting of the curriculum, attending class daily and doing all the class activities, homework, and POWs. Because of this experience, her contributions to focus groups had a unique perspective. This is a good place to thank her also for her contributions to IMP as Network Coordinator for California. In that capacity, she has visited many IMP classrooms and answered thousands of questions from parents, teachers, and administrators.

- **Lori Green** left the classroom as a regular teacher after the 1989–90 school year and became a traveling resource for IMP classroom teachers. In that role, she has seen more classes using the curriculum than we can count, and the insights from her classroom observations have been a valuable resource in her work in the focus groups.

- **Celia Stevenson** developed the charming and witty graphics that graced the pre-publication versions of all the IMP units.

Several people played particular roles in the development of this unit, *The Pit and the Pendulum:*

- Matt Bremer, Janice Bussey, Donna Gaarder, Lori Green, and Tom Zimmerman helped us create the version of *The Pit and the Pendulum* that was pilot tested during 1989–90. They not only taught the unit in their classrooms that year, but also read and commented on early drafts, tested out almost all the activities during workshops that preceded the teaching, and then came back after teaching the unit with insights that contributed to the initial revision.

- Dean Ballard, Dan Johnson, and Greg Smith joined Matt Bremer, Mary Jo Cittadino, and Lori Green for the focus group on *The Pit and the Pendulum* in September, 1993. Their contributions built on several years of IMP teaching, including at least two years teaching this unit, and their work led to the development of the last field-test version of the unit.

- Dan Branham, Dave Calhoun, John Chart, Steve Hansen, Mary Hunter, Caran Resciniti, Gwennyth Trice, and Julie Walker field tested the post-focus group version of *The Pit and the Pendulum* during 1994–95. Dave and John met with us when the teaching of the unit was finished to share their experiences. Their feedback helped shape the final version that now appears.

In creating this program, we needed help in many dimensions other than writing curriculum and giving support to teachers.

The National Science Foundation has been the primary sponsor of the Interactive Mathematics Program. We want to thank NSF for its ongoing support, and especially want to extend our personal thanks to Dr. Margaret Cozzens, Director of NSF's Division of Elementary, Secondary, and Informal Education, for her encouragement and her faith in our efforts.

We also want to acknowledge here the initial support for curriculum development from the California Postsecondary Education Commission and the San Francisco Foundation, and the major support for dissemination from the Noyce Foundation and the David and Lucile Packard Foundation.

Keeping all of our work going required the help of a first-rate office staff. This group of talented and hard-working individuals worked tirelessly on many tasks, such as sending out units, keeping the books balanced, helping us get our message out to the public, and handling communications with schools, teachers, and administrators. We greatly appreciate their dedication.

- Barbara Ford—Secretary

- Tony Gillies—Project Manager

- Marianne Smith—Publicist

- Linda Witnov—Outreach Coordinator

We want to thank Dr. Norman Webb, of the Wisconsin Center for Education Research, for his leadership in our evaluation program, and our Evaluation Advisory Board, whose expertise was so valuable in that aspect of our work.

- David Clarke, University of Melbourne

- Robert Davis, Rutgers University

- George Hein, Lesley College

- Mark St. John, Inverness Research Associates

Finally, we want to thank Steve Rasmussen, President of Key Curriculum Press, Casey FitzSimons, Key's Project Editor for the IMP curriculum, and the many others at Key whose work turned our ideas and words into published form.

Dan Fendel   Diane Resek   Lynne Alper   Sherry Fraser

The Interactive Mathematics Program

What is the Interactive Mathematics Program?

The Interactive Mathematics Program (IMP) is a growing collaboration of mathematicians, teacher-educators, and teachers who have been working together since 1989 on both curriculum development and teacher professional development.

What is the IMP curriculum?

IMP has created a four-year program of problem-based mathematics that replaces the traditional Algebra I–Geometry–Algebra II/Trigonometry–Precalculus sequence and that is designed to exemplify the curriculum reform called for in the *Curriculum and Evaluation Standards* of the National Council of Teachers of Mathematics.

The IMP curriculum integrates traditional material with additional topics recommended by the NCTM *Standards*, such as statistics, probability, curve fitting, and matrix algebra. Although every IMP unit has a specific mathematical focus (for instance, similar triangles), most units are structured around a central problem and bring in other topics as needed to solve that problem, rather than narrowly restricting the mathematical content. Ideas that are developed in one unit are generally revisited and deepened in one or more later units.

For which students is the IMP curriculum intended?

The IMP curriculum is for all students. One of IMP's goals is to make the learning of a core mathematics curriculum accessible to everyone. Toward that end, we have designed the program for use with heterogeneous classes. We provide you with a varied collection of supplemental problems to give you the flexibility to meet individual student needs.

Teacher Phyllis Quick confers with a group of students.

How is the IMP classroom different?

When you use the IMP curriculum, your role changes from "imparter of knowledge" to observer and facilitator. You ask challenging questions. You do not give all the answers but you prod students to do their own thinking, to make generalizations, and to go beyond the immediate problem by asking themselves "What if?"

The IMP curriculum gives students many opportunities to write about their mathematical thinking, to reflect on what they have done, and to make oral presentations to each other about their work. In IMP, your assessment of students becomes integrated with learning, and you evaluate students in a variety of ways, including class participation, daily homework assignments, Problems of the Week, portfolios, and unit assessments. The IMP *Teaching Handbook* provides many practical suggestions for teachers on how to get the best possible results using this curriculum in *your* classroom.

What is in Year 1 of the IMP curriculum?

Year 1 of the IMP curriculum contains five units.

Patterns

The primary purpose of this unit is to introduce students to ways of working on and thinking about mathematics that may be new to them. In a sense, the unit is an overall introduction to the IMP curriculum, which involves changes for many students in how they learn mathematics and what they think of as mathematics. The main mathematical ideas of the unit include function tables, the use of variables, positive and negative numbers, and some basic geometrical concepts.

The Game of Pig

A dice game called Pig forms the core of this unit. Playing and analyzing Pig involves students in a wide variety of mathematical activities. The basic problem for students is to find an optimum strategy for playing the game. In order to find a good strategy and prove that it is optimum, students work with the concept of expected value and develop a mathematical analysis for the game based on an area model for probability.

The Overland Trail

This unit looks at the mid-nineteenth century western migration across what is now the United States in terms of the many mathematical relationships involved. These relationships involve planning what to take on the 2400-mile trek, estimating the cost of the move, studying rates of consumption and of travel, and estimating the time to reach the final goal. A major mathematical focus of the unit is the use of equations, tables, and graphs to describe real-life situations.

The Pit and the Pendulum

In Edgar Allan Poe's story, *The Pit and the Pendulum,* a prisoner is tied down while a pendulum with a sharp blade slowly descends. If the prisoner does not act, he will be killed by the pendulum. Students read an excerpt from the story, and are presented with the problem of whether the prisoner would have enough time to escape. To resolve this question, they construct pendulums and conduct experiments. In the process, they are introduced to the concepts of normal distribution and standard deviation as tools for determining whether a change in one variable really does affect another. They use graphing calculators to learn about quadratic equations and to explore curve fitting. Finally, after deriving a theoretical answer to the pendulum problem, students actually build a thirty-foot pendulum to test their theory.

Shadows

The central question of this unit is, "How can you predict the length of a shadow?" The unit moves quickly from this concrete problem to the geometric concept of similarity. Students work with a variety of approaches to come to an understanding of similar polygons, especially similar triangles. Then they return to the problem of the shadow, applying their knowledge of similar triangles and using informal methods for solving proportions, to develop a general formula. In the last part of the unit, students learn about the three primary trigonometric functions—sine, cosine, and tangent—as they apply to acute angles, and they apply these functions to problems of finding heights and distances.

How do the four years of the IMP curriculum fit together?

The four years of the IMP curriculum form an integrated sequence through which students can learn the mathematics they will need, both for further education and on the job. Although the organization of the IMP curriculum is very different from the traditional Algebra I–Geometry–Algebra II/Trigonometry–Precalculus sequence, the important mathematical ideas are all there.

Here are some examples of how both traditional concepts and topics new to the high school curriculum are developed.

Linear equations

In Year 1 of the IMP curriculum, students develop an intuitive foundation about algebraic thinking, including the use of variables, which they build on throughout the program. In the Year 2 unit *Solve It!,* students use the concept of equivalent equations to see how to solve any linear equation in a single variable. Later in Year 2, in a unit called *Cookies* (about maximizing profits for a bakery), they solve pairs of linear equations in two variables, using both algebraic and geometric methods. In the Year 3 unit *Meadows or Malls?,* they extend those ideas to systems with more than two variables, and see how to use matrices and the technology of graphing calculators to solve such systems.

Measurement and the Pythagorean theorem

Measurement, including area and volume, is one of the fundamental topics in geometry. The Pythagorean theorem is one of the most important geometric principles ever discovered. In the Year 2 unit *Do Bees Build It Best?,* students combine these ideas with their knowledge of similarity (from the Year 1 unit *Shadows*) to see why the hexagonal prism of the bees' honeycomb design is the most efficient regular prism possible. Students also use the Pythagorean theorem in later units, applying it to develop principles like the distance formula in coordinate geometry.

Trigonometric functions

In traditional programs, the trigonometric functions are introduced in the eleventh or twelfth grade. In the IMP curriculum, students begin working with trigonometry in Year 1 (in *Shadows*), using right-triangle trigonometry in several units (including *Do Bees Build It Best?*) in Years 2 and 3. In the Year 4 unit *High Dive,* they extend trigonometry from right triangles to circular functions, in the context of a circus act in which a performer falls from a Ferris wheel into a moving tub of water. (In *High Dive,* students also learn principles of physics, developing laws for falling objects and finding the vertical and horizontal components of velocity.)

Standard deviation and the binomial distribution

Standard deviation and the binomial distribution are major tools in the study of probability and statistics. *The Game of Pig* gets students started by building a firm understanding of concepts of probability and the phenomenon of experimental variation. Later in Year 1 (in *The Pit and the Pendulum*), they use standard deviation to see that the period of a pendulum is determined primarily by its length. In Year 2, they compare standard deviation with the chi-square test in examining whether a set of data is statistically significant. In *Pennant Fever* (Year 3), students use the binomial distribution to evaluate a team's chances of winning the baseball championship, and in *The Pollster's Dilemma* (Year 4), students tie many of these ideas together in the central limit theorem, seeing how the margin of error and the level of certainty for an election poll depend on its size.

Does the program work?

The IMP curriculum has been thoroughly field-tested by hundreds of classroom teachers around the country. Their enthusiasm comes from the success they have seen in their own classrooms with their own students. For those who measure success by test scores, we mention that repeated studies have proved that IMP students do at least as well as students in traditional mathematics classes on tests like the SAT, even though IMP students spend far less time than traditional students on the algebra and geometry skills emphasized by these tests. With the time saved, IMP students learn topics such as statistics that other students don't see until they reach college.

But one of our proudest achievements is that IMP students are excited about mathematics, as shown by the fact that they take more mathematics courses in high school than their counterparts in traditional programs. We think this is because they see that mathematics can be relevant to their own lives. If so, then the program works.

Dan Fendel
Diane Resek
Lynne Alper
Sherry Fraser

Note to Students

These pages in the student book welcome students to the program.

You are about to begin an adventure in mathematics, an adventure organized around interesting, complex problems. The concepts you learn grow out of what is needed to solve those problems.

This curriculum was developed by the Interactive Mathematics Program (IMP), a collaboration of teachers, teacher-educators, and mathematicians who have been working together since 1989 to reform the way high school mathematics is taught. About one hundred thousand students and five hundred teachers used these materials before they were published. Their experiences, reactions, and ideas have been incorporated into the final version you now hold.

Our goal is to give you the mathematics you need to succeed in this changing world. We want to present mathematics to you in a manner that reflects how mathematics is used and reflects the different ways people work and learn together. Through this perspective on mathematics, you will be prepared both for continued study of mathematics in college and for the world of work.

This book contains the various assignments that will be your work during Year 1 of the program. As you will see, these assignments incorporate ideas from many branches of mathematics, including algebra, geometry, probability, graphing, statistics, and trigonometry. Other topics will come up in later parts of this four-year program. Rather than present each of these areas separately, we have integrated them and presented them in meaningful contexts so that you'll see how they relate to one another and to our world.

Each unit in this four-year program has a central problem or theme, and focuses on several major mathematical ideas. Within each unit, the material is organized for teaching purposes into "Days," with a homework assignment for each day. (Your class may not follow this schedule exactly, especially if it doesn't meet every day.)

At the end of the main material for each unit, you will find a set of "supplemental problems." These problems provide additional opportunities for you to work with ideas from the unit, either to strengthen your understanding of the core material or to explore new ideas related to the unit.

Although the IMP program is not organized into courses called Algebra, Geometry, and so on, you will be learning all the essential mathematical concepts that are part of those traditional courses. You will also be learning concepts from branches of mathematics—especially statistics and probability—that are not part of a traditional high school program.

To accomplish this goal, you will have to be an active learner. Simply reading this book will not allow you to achieve your goal, because the book does not teach directly. Your role as a mathematics student will be to experiment, investigate, ask questions, make and test conjectures, and reflect, and then communicate your ideas and conclusions both verbally and in writing. You will do some work in collaboration with your fellow students, just as users of mathematics in the real world often work in teams. At other times, you will be working on your own.

We hope you will enjoy the challenge of this new way of learning mathematics and will see mathematics in a new light.

Dan Fendel   Diane Resek   Lynne Alper   Sherry Fraser

Finding What You Need

We designed this guide to help you find what you need amid all the information it provides. Each of the following components has a special treatment in the layout of the guide.

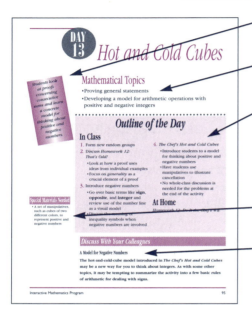

Synopsis of the Day: The key idea or activity for each day is summarized in a brief sentence or two.

Mathematical Topics: Mathematical issues for the day are presented in a bulleted list.

Outline of the Day: Under the *In Class* heading, the outline summarizes the activities for the day, which are keyed to numbered headings in the discussion. Daily homework assignments and Problems of the Week are listed under the *At Home* heading.

Special Materials Needed: Special items needed in the classroom for each day are bulleted here.

Discuss With Your Colleagues: This section highlights topics that you may want to discuss with your peers.

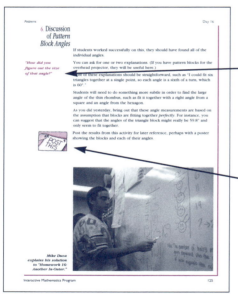

Suggested Questions: These are specific questions that you might ask during an activity or discussion to promote student insight or to determine whether students understand an idea. The appropriateness of these questions generally depends on what students have already developed or presented on their own.

Post This: The *Post This* icon indicates items that you may want to display in the classroom.

Icons for Student Written Products

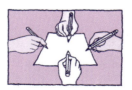

Single Group report

Individual reports

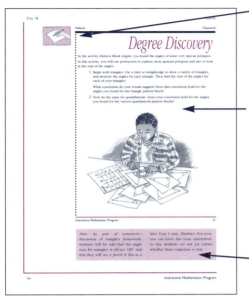

Icons for Student Written Products: For each group activity, there is an icon suggesting a single group report, individual reports, or no report at all. If graphs are included, the icon indicates this as well. (The graph icons do not appear in every unit.)

Embedded Student Pages: Embedded within the pages of the teacher guide are reduced-size copies of the pages from the student book. These reduced student pages include the "transition pages" that appear occasionally within each unit to summarize each portion of the unit and to prepare students for what is coming. Having all of these student pages in the teacher guide is a helpful way for you to see things from the students' perspective.

Asides: These are ideas outside the main thrust of a discussion. They include background information for teachers, refinements or subtle points that may only be of interest to some students, ways to help fill in gaps in understanding the main ideas, and suggestions about when to bring in a particular concept.

Additional Information

Here is a brief outline of other tools we have included to assist you and make both the teaching and the learning experience more rewarding.

Glossary: This section, which is found at the back of the book, gives the definitions of important terms for all of Year 1 for easy reference. The same glossary appears in the student book.

Appendix A: Supplemental Problems: This appendix contains a variety of interesting additional activities for the unit, for teachers who would like to supplement material found in the regular classroom problems. These additional activities are of two types—*reinforcements,* which help increase student understanding of concepts that are central to the unit, and *extensions,* which allow students to explore ideas beyond the basic unit.

Appendix B: Blackline Masters: For each unit, this appendix contains materials you can reproduce that are not available in the student book and that will be helpful to teacher and student alike. They include the end-of-unit assessments as well as such items as diagrams from which you can make transparencies. Semester assessments for Year 1 are included in *The Overland Trail* (for first semester) and *Shadows* (for second semester).

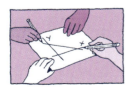

Single group graph

Individual graphs

No report at all

Year 1 IMP Units

Patterns

The Game of Pig

The Overland Trail

The Pit and the Pendulum (in this book)

Shadows

Contents

"*The Pit and the Pendulum*" *Overview*

Summary of the Unit

This unit opens with an excerpt from Edgar Allan Poe's classic short story "The Pit and the Pendulum." In the story, a prisoner is tied down while a pendulum with a sharp blade slowly descends. If the prisoner does not act, he will be killed by the swinging blade. At a point when the pendulum seems to have about 12 swings left and is about 30 feet long, the prisoner creates a plan for escape and executes it, apparently taking a little more than a minute to do so.

Students are first presented with the question of whether Poe's story is realistic. After some discussion, the question then becomes "How long would it take for Poe's pendulum to make 12 swings?"

In order to analyze this question, students need to decide what variables are worth paying attention to. After conducting some initial pendulum experiments to get a feel for the situation, they do a series of experiments involving other phenomena that bring up problems of measurement variation and precision. They see that the precision of a measurement depends on the tools used to do the measuring, but they also see that even under optimal conditions—measuring the same thing twice in the same way—one will not necessarily get the same answer each time.

This finding leads to a realization that differences in the period measurements between different pendulums may be only accidental, and not related to the differences between the pendulums.

As part of the development of this idea, the unit presents the concept of *normal distribution,* together with some basic facts about such distributions. Students learn that taking many measurements of a given phenomenon generally results in a set of values that are normally distributed.

Then students look informally at issues of data spread, developing their own ideas of how spread might be measured. They learn about the concept of *standard deviation* and see how it is used to determine what variation in measurements of a phenomenon is "ordinary" and what is "rare."

Students use standard deviation to decide which variables are important in predicting the period of a pendulum swing. Eventually, they conclude that the period of a pendulum is determined, at least primarily, by its length.

The last stage of the analysis is to predict the period of a 30-foot pendulum. After an open-ended exploration of graphs of different functions, students collect data about shorter pendulums of various lengths. It turns out that the data set is not linear, that is, the graph is not a straight line. The non-linearity makes extrapolation somewhat difficult.

Students then use what they have learned about graphs. Applying curve-fitting techniques on the graphing calculator, they plot the data they found relating the period of a pendulum to its length and find a function whose graph passes close to all of their plotted points. They then use this function to predict how long it will take a 30-foot pendulum to make twelve swings.

Finally, to check their prediction, they actually build a 30-foot pendulum and measure the period directly.

The content of the unit can be outlined like this:

- Days 1–3: Introduction of the problem and initial experiments
- Days 4–6: Measurement variation and study of data from repeated measurements; POW 12 presentations
- Days 7–9: Normal distribution
- Day 10: Mini-POW in connection with POW 13
- Days 11–15: Data spread and standard deviation
- Day 16: Collecting and analyzing data from many measurements of a standard pendulum
- Days 17–18: Determining which variables affect the period of a pendulum
- Days 19–20: POW sharing and presentations of POW 14
- Days 21–24: Graphs and their equations
- Days 25: Collection of data on periods for pendulums with different lengths
- Day 26: Curve fitting with the pendulum data and prediction for a 30-foot pendulum
- Day 27: Building a 30-foot pendulum and checking predictions
- Day 28: POW 15 presentations and assembling of portfolios

The final two days of the unit are for end-of-unit assessments and summing up.

Concepts and Skills

This unit blends scientific experiments with the statistical concepts of normal distribution and standard deviation and the algebra of functions and graphs.

The main concepts and skills that students will encounter and practice during the course of this unit can be summarized by category as shown below.

Experiments and data

- Planning and performing controlled scientific experiments
- Working with the concept of period
- Recognizing the phenomenon of measurement variation
- Collecting and analyzing data
- Expressing experimental results and other data using frequency bar graphs

Statistics

- Learning about the normal distribution
- Making area estimates to understand the normal distribution
- Developing concepts of data spread, especially standard deviation
- Working with symmetry and concavity in connection with the normal distribution and standard deviation
- Using standard deviation and the normal distribution in problem contexts
- Distinguishing between standard deviation and sample standard deviation
- Calculating the mean and standard deviation of data, both by hand and with calculators
- Using standard deviation to decide whether a variation in experiment results is significant

Functions and graphs

- Using function notation
- Using graphing calculators to explore the graphs of different functions
- Fitting a function to data using a graphing calculator
- Making predictions based on curve fitting

Other concepts and skills are developed in connection with Problems of the Week.

Materials

You will need to provide special materials during this unit (in addition to standard materials such as graphing calculators, transparencies, chart paper, marking pens, and so on).

A complete set of materials for pendulum experiments should be available to students at various times during the unit. We will refer to these items as **experiment materials** when they are specifically needed. Here is a list of the experiment materials.

- Unwaxed dental floss (about 400 feet)
- Rulers or meter sticks (two per group)
- Paper clips (several per group)
- Masking tape
- Heavy washers, all of the same size and shape (about 15 per group)
- Stopwatches (one per group)
- Protractors (one per group)
- Scissors (one per group)

Also provide an assortment of other materials, such as different kinds of string or objects of different sizes and shapes to use as weights, so that students can vary their experiments.

You can give students easy access to these experiment materials in your classroom by placing sets of the materials in shoe boxes or baskets (one per group).

In addition to the experiment materials, you will need to provide these items for other specific activities:

- Beans or other manipulatives for counting (at least 45 per pair of students)
- (Optional) A ladder (in order to test long pendulums in class)
- Materials to make a 30-foot pendulum

Grading

The IMP *Teaching Handbook* contains general ideas about how to grade students in an IMP class. You will probably want to check daily that students have done their homework, and include the regular completion of homework as part of students' grades. Your grading scheme will probably also include Problems of the Week, the unit portfolio, and the end-of-unit assessments.

Because you will not be able to read thoroughly every assignment that students turn in, you will need to select certain assignments to read carefully and to base grades on. Here are some suggestions.

- *Initial Experiments* (evaluating the quality of student's group work during Days 2 and 3; you will need to observe students carefully in their groups during these two days).

- *Homework 5: Pulse Analysis*

- *Homework 11: Dinky and Minky Spread Data*

- *Homework 14: Penny Weight Revisited*

- *Homework 18: Pendulum Conclusions* (using students' grades for each other)

- *Homework 24: Graphing Summary* (summarizing conclusions from the activity for Days 22–24, *Graphing Free-for-All*)

- *Homework 26: Mathematics and Science*

If you want to base your grading on a larger number of tasks, there are many other homework assignments, class activities, and oral presentations you can use.

Interactive Mathematics Program

IMP

Integrated High School Mathematics

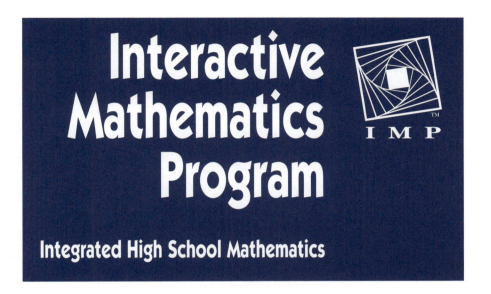

YEAR 1

The Pit and the Pendulum

The Pit and the Pendulum

Days 1-6

Edgar Allan Poe—Master of Suspense

The title of this unit comes from a short story by Edgar Allan Poe, who wrote poetry and fiction in the first half of the nineteenth century. (Probably some of the folks on the Overland Trail were readers of Poe.)

Many of his stories involve mystery, suspense, and the bizarre, and *The Pit and the Pendulum* is no exception.

This page in the student book introduces Days 1 through 6.

Lindsay Crawford and Catherine Bartz work on their group's initial experiments.

Interactive Mathematics Program   307

Escape from the Pit

Students read an excerpt from Poe's story "The Pit and the Pendulum" and define the unit problem.

Mathematical Topics

- Deciding what information is relevant to the solution of a problem
- Concept of **period**

Outline of the Day

In Class

1. Form random groups, and remind students that they need scientific calculators for use at home
2. Have students read the excerpt from Poe's "The Pit and the Pendulum"
3. *The Question*
   - Students examine the excerpt and look for information about whether the prisoner had time to escape

4. Discuss *The Question*
   - Bring out relevant facts in the excerpt
   - State and post "The Revised Question"
   - Introduce the term *period*

At Home

Homework 1: Building a Pendulum

POW 12: The Big Knight Switch (due Day 6)

Discuss With Your Colleagues

It's Not in Their Vocabulary

A number of words in Poe's story are not in the vocabulary of high school students (or even of most adults). Yet, if you stop to define these words before or during your reading of the story, some of the excitement of hearing the story will be lost.

Reflect on how you have learned new vocabulary. Was it ever through reading in context? Discuss whether you need to understand each word in order to understand a story. Finally, discuss the change in atmosphere when you introduce the definition of words into the reading of a story.

1. Forming Groups

At the beginning of the unit, put students into new groups as described in the IMP *Teaching Handbook.* We recommend that you create new groups again on Day 10 and on Day 20.

• *Calculator reminder*

On Day 1 of *Patterns,* students should have been told that they need to provide their own scientific calculators for use at home. This unit is the first one for which they will actually need more than a four-function calculator.

Tell students who have not yet made this purchase that they will find it extremely helpful to have a calculator with statistical capability when they get to *Homework 16: Standard Pendulum Data and Decisions.*

Note: Students will also need trigonometric functions on their calculator in the next unit, *Shadows.*

Ben Snyder makes notes as he reads the excerpt from Poe's "The Pit and the Pendulum."

The Pit and the Pendulum

Excerpts from
"The Pit and the Pendulum"
by Edgar Allan Poe (1809-1849)

. . . Looking upward, I surveyed the ceiling of my prison. It was some thirty or forty feet overhead, and constructed much as the side walls. In one of its panels a very singular figure riveted my whole attention. It was the painted picture of Time as he is commonly represented, save that, in lieu of a scythe, he held what, at a casual glance, I supposed to be the pictured image of a huge pendulum such as we see on antique clocks. There was something, however, in the appearance of this machine which caused me to regard it more attentively. While I gazed directly upward at it (for its position was immediately over my own) I fancied that I saw it in motion. In an instant afterward the fancy was confirmed. Its sweep was brief, and of course slow. I watched it for some minutes, somewhat in fear, but more in wonder. Wearied at length with observing its dull movement, I turned my eyes upon the other objects in the cell. . . .

It might have been half an hour, perhaps even an hour, (for I could take but imperfect note of time) before I again cast my eyes upward. What I then saw confounded and amazed me. The sweep of the pendulum had increased in extent by nearly a yard. As a natural consequence its velocity was also much greater. But what mainly disturbed me was the idea that it had perceptibly *descended*. I now observed—with what horror it is needless to say—that its nether extremity was formed of a crescent of glittering steel, about a foot in length from horn to horn; the horns upward, and the under edge evidently as keen as that of a razor. Like a razor also, it seemed massy and heavy, tapering from the edge into a solid and broad structure above. It was appended to a weighty rod of brass, and the whole *hissed* as it swung through the air. . . .

What boots it to tell of the long, long hours of horror more than mortal, during which I counted the rushing oscillations of the steel! Inch by inch—line by line—with a descent only appreciable at intervals that seemed ages—down and still down it came! . . .

Continued on next page

2. The Story: *The Pit and the Pendulum*

Read the excerpts from the story to the class or ask students to take turns reading aloud. Don't worry if students don't understand every word of the

The vibration of the pendulum was at right angles to my length. I saw that the crescent was designed to cross the region of the heart. It would fray the serge of my robe—it would return and repeat its operation—again—and again....

Down—steadily down it crept....

Down—certainly, relentlessly down! It vibrated within three inches of my bosom! . . .

I saw that some ten or twelve vibrations would bring the steel in actual contact with my robe, and with this observation there suddenly came over my spirit all the keen, collected calmness of despair. For the first time during many hours—or perhaps days— I *thought*. It now occurred to me, that the bandage, or surcingle, which enveloped me, was *unique*. I was tied by no separate cord. The first stroke of the razor-like crescent athwart any portion of the band, would so detach it that it might be unwound from my person by means of my left hand. But how fearful, in that case, the proximity of the steel! The result of the slightest struggle how deadly! Was it likely, moreover, that the minions of the torturer had not foreseen and provided for this possibility? Was it probable that the bandage crossed my bosom in the track of the pendulum? Dreading to find my faint, and, as it seemed, my last hope frustrated, I so far elevated my head as to obtain a distinct view of my breast. The surcingle enveloped my limbs and body close in all directions—*save in the path of the destroying crescent*.

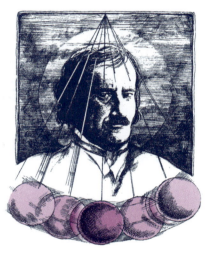

Scarcely had I dropped my head back into its original position, when there flashed upon my mind what I cannot better describe than as the unformed half of that idea of deliverance to which I have previously alluded, and of which a moiety only floated indeterminately through my brain when I raised food to my burning lips. The whole thought was now present—feeble, scarcely sane, scarcely definite,—but still entire. I proceeded at once, with the nervous energy of despair, to attempt its execution.

Continued on next page

story; the important thing is that they get a general sense of what is going on. There is no need to define vocabulary from the story before reading— students will derive meaning from the context.

You may want to mention that the story was written about 150 years ago.

For many hours the immediate vicinity of the low framework upon which I lay, had been literally swarming with rats. They were wild, bold, ravenous; their red eyes glaring upon me as if they waited but for motionlessness on my part to make me their prey. "To what food," I thought, "have they been accustomed in the well?"

They had devoured, in spite of all my efforts to prevent them, all but a small remnant of the contents of the dish. I had fallen into an habitual see-saw, or wave of the hand about the platter; and, at length, the unconscious uniformity of the movement deprived it of effect. In their voracity the vermin frequently fastened their sharp fangs in my fingers. With the particles of the oily and spicy viand which now remained, I thoroughly rubbed the bandage wherever I could reach it; then, raising my hand from the floor, I lay breathlessly still.

At first the ravenous animals were startled and terrified at the change—at the cessation of movement. They shrank alarmedly back; many sought the well. But this was only for a moment. I had not counted in vain upon their voracity. Observing that I remained without motion, one or two of the boldest leaped upon the framework, and smelt at the surcingle. This seemed the signal for a general rush. Forth from the well they hurried in fresh troops. They clung to the wood—they overran it, and leaped in hundreds upon my person. The measured movement of the pendulum disturbed them not at all. Avoiding its strokes they busied themselves with the anointed bandage. They pressed—they swarmed upon me in ever accumulating heaps. They writhed upon my throat; their cold lips sought my own; I was half stifled by their thronging pressure; disgust, for which the world has no name, swelled my bosom, and chilled, with a heavy clamminess, my heart. Yet one minute, and I felt that the struggle would be over. Plainly I perceived the loosening of the bandage. I knew that in more than one place it must be already severed. With a more than human resolution I lay *still*.

Nor had I erred in my calculations—nor had I endured in vain. I at length felt that I was *free*. The surcingle hung in ribands from my body. But the stroke of the pendulum already pressed upon my bosom. It had divided the serge of the robe. It had cut through the linen beneath. Twice again it swung, and a sharp sense of pain shot through every nerve. But the moment of escape had arrived. At a wave of my hand my deliverers hurried tumultuously away. With a steady movement—cautious, sidelong, shrinking, and slow—I slid from the embrace of the bandage and beyond the reach of the scimitar. For the moment, at least, *I was free*.

The Question

The initial question of this unit is

Does the story's hero really have time to carry out his escape plan?

1. Based on the information you have, draw your own sketch of the prisoner's situation.

2. Next, go back through the story and carefully search for any additional information about the pendulum and the time for the prisoner's escape. Compile a group list of any information you find. If you are uncertain about the importance or relevance of a piece of information, write it down—you may need it later. Also write down any questions you have and identify any information you wish you had.

3. In your group, share your initial opinions about the question stated above.

3. *The Question*

Note: Be sure to leave enough time for discussion of this activity, brainstorming for the homework, and introduction of the POW.

After students have read the selection, have them turn to *The Question*. This activity asks students to go through the story looking for information that pertains to the pendulum and to the time for the prisoner's escape.

Tell them that the club card student in each group will be the spokesperson.

4. Discussion of *The Question*

"What is one of your findings or one of your questions?"

Ask each group to report one of its findings or questions.

You can make two lists on chart paper from their responses.

- What students know

- What students need to find out

Keep going back to the groups in turn until their lists are exhausted.

Several specific pieces of information should be noted. If students do not see them, you should point them out.

- The ceiling is "some thirty or forty feet overhead" (1st paragraph), so the pendulum is likely to be about this long.

- The pendulum is "within three inches of my bosom" (6th paragraph) when the prisoner develops his plan.

- The pendulum needs "some ten or twelve vibrations" (7th paragraph) before it reaches him.

- "Yet one minute" (near the end of the next-to-last paragraph) is all that is needed until the bandage would be loosened by the rats.

This discussion should also bring out the fact that the story may not give students all the information they need. Explain that, in order to give the initial question some direction and specificity, they need to make some assumptions.

For example, since they are interested only in the last few swings of the pendulum, they can ignore the fact that the blade is moving down and that the length is changing.

Tell students that this unit will use 30 feet as the length (from Poe's "some thirty or forty feet overhead") and 12 swings as the duration (from Poe's "some ten or twelve vibrations"). However, there may be other assumptions needed later. Thus, for now, the unit will look at the following narrower question:

> The Revised Question
>
> *How long would it take for Poe's pendulum to make 12 swings?*

Post this question on the wall in the classroom, since students will be working on it, with some digressions, for the rest of the unit. Leave room under the question to write an outline of steps for answering it. Students will add to the outline as the unit progresses.

Introduce the term **period** for the amount of time it takes for a pendulum to make a complete swing (back *and* forth).

Tell the class that the basic goal of the unit will be to answer this revised question. Ask students:

*"What information
and materials do
you need to answer
the unit question?"*

• What information do you need to answer this new question?

• How can you get that information?

• What materials will you need?

If students suggest that they simply construct a pendulum like Poe's, tell them that they will eventually do so. However, you should ask them if they really have enough information at this point to construct a full-scale model of the pendulum. In particular, they don't yet know which facts about the pendulum are important.

Tell students that the unit focuses on trying to devise an indirect method to answer the revised question (that is, a method other than building the pendulum). Their task is to use mathematics to find the answer.

Homework 1:
Building a
Pendulum
(see facing page)

*"How could you
build a pendulum
at home?"*

You may want to have students brainstorm about how to build the pendulum called for in this assignment. Tell the class that their pendulums need not be elaborate.

Homework 1 Building a Pendulum

1. Tell the story of "The Pit and the Pendulum" to a family member, friend, or neighbor. Ask the listener if the time for the prisoner's escape plan seems realistic and how you could find out if it is.

2. Write about these topics.

   a. What were the reactions of your listener?

   b. Did the listener think the amount of time in the story seemed realistic? What was the listener's reasoning?

   c. How did the listener think you could find out how realistic this time estimate was?

3. Make a pendulum from materials that you find around your house.

4. Figure out a way to measure the period of your pendulum as accurately as you can. (Working with the family member, friend, or neighbor on this may be helpful.) *Remember:* The period is the time it takes for your pendulum to swing back *and* forth once.

5. Write about how you measured the period.

6. Bring your pendulum to class with you tomorrow.

POW 12   *The Big Knight Switch*

Strict rules determine how knight pieces may move on a chessboard. Each "move" consists of two squares in one direction and then one square in a perpendicular direction.

For example, knights may move forward (or backward) two squares and then to the right (or left) one square, as shown in A below; similarly, they may move to the left (or right) two squares and then down (or up) one square, as shown in B below.

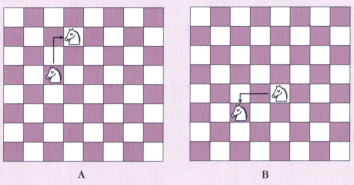

A   B

The rules also state that no two chess pieces may occupy the same square at the same time, although knights may pass or jump over other pieces on the way to an empty square.

That's it—there are no other choices. So knights can get pretty bored spending their days on the chessboard.

One day two black knights and two white knights were sitting around on a 3-by-3 chessboard, just as you see below, feeling restless.

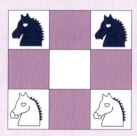

Continued on next page

Interactive Mathematics Program   313

POW 12: The Big Knight Switch

You may want to discuss in class how the knight piece moves on a chessboard to be sure that students understand it. This POW is scheduled to be presented on Day 6.

To liven things up, they decided to try to switch places, so that the white knights would end up where the black knights started out, and vice versa. Unfortunately, they could move only one at a time, according to the rules described above, and they had to stay within the nine squares of their board.

The big questions (to keep you from being bored) are:

1. Can they do it?

2. If so, what is the least number of moves it will take them to switch, and how do you know this number is the least?

3. If it is not possible, explain why not.

Reminder: Save your notes as you work on the problem. You will need them to do your write-up.

Write-up

1. *Problem statement*

2. *Process:* Be sure to include a description of how you kept track of the various moves. Also describe the different approaches you used to working on the problem.

3. *Solution:* Be sure to explain why you think your answer represents the least possible number of moves or why you think the task is impossible.

4. *Extensions*

5. *Evaluation*

Adapted from *aha! Insight*, by Martin Gardner, Scientific American, Inc./W. H. Freeman and Company, San Francisco, © 1978.

Initial Experiments

Mathematical Topics

- Comparing methods for measuring period
- Brainstorming about factors that may influence the period of a pendulum
- Devising an experiment

Outline of the Day

In Class

1. Discuss *Homework 1: Building a Pendulum*
2. Describe the general plan for answering the revised question
   - Post this outline, leaving room for more details as the unit progresses
3. Brainstorm and post a list of variables that might affect the period of a pendulum
4. Discuss the importance of group work
   - Develop and post criteria for a successful group

5. *Initial Experiments*
   - Students perform preliminary experiments to study what affects the period of a pendulum
   - The activity will be completed and discussed on Day 3

At Home

Homework 2: Close to the Law

Special Materials Needed

- Experiment materials (see list in *Overview*)

Discuss With Your Colleagues

Managing a Science Class

When students work on experiments during this unit, you will need to manage equipment as well as the groups of students.

Discuss techniques for both kinds of management. What issues might arise? You may want to get advice from some science teachers.

1. Discussion of Homework 1: Building a Pendulum

Have several students share with the class their homework experience from the night before. Discuss the problems they had in measuring the period.

"How did you measure the period of your pendulum?"

Ask students to tell what methods they used for measuring a period. For example, some may have timed several swings and then divided by the number of swings. Others may have measured several individual swings and then averaged the results.

There is no single best way to measure, for there are pros and cons to each method. For example, it is easier to make a single measurement of the time required for several swings than to do several measurements of one swing at a time. On the other hand, a student could argue that timing several swings in one measurement is not a valid method because the pendulum gradually slows down.

Note: If students do not have different approaches, there is no need to pursue this issue now. The importance of the issue will be examined in the Day 5 discussion of *Homework 4: What's Your Stride?*

2. The General Plan

"What is the central question of the unit?"

Remind students that in order to answer the initial question ("Does the story's hero really have time to carry out his escape plan?"), they must consider the narrower question that was posted yesterday.

The Revised Question

> *How long would it take for Poe's pendulum to make 12 swings?*

Tell students that, in order to answer this revised question, they will need to follow these steps.

1. Find out which variable or variables affect the period of the pendulum.

2. Collect data on the periods of various pendulums, changing only the variable(s) decided on in step 1.

3. Look for patterns in the data and use the patterns to predict how long the 12 swings of Poe's pendulum will take.

Post this outline so students can refer to it throughout the unit. They will be adding further details to the outline over the course of the unit. You may find it helpful to put each item of the outline on a sentence strip so you can make insertions as needed.

3. Brainstorming About Variables

"What might affect the period of a pendulum?"

Give groups some time to make a list of potentially relevant variables—that is, of all the things that they think might influence the period of a pendulum.

Then have the diamond card member of each group state one of the group's proposed variables. From these reports, make and post a class list of things that might influence the period of a pendulum. You will probably want to introduce the term **bob** for the weight at the end of the pendulum.

Here are some possibilities the class might come up with.

- Weight of the bob

- Length of the string

- Distance the pendulum bob is pulled back (this is called its **initial amplitude**)

- Composition of the bob (what it is made of)

- Shape of the bob

- Composition and weight of the string

4. Group Work and Assessment

Tell students that, in the next activity, they will be working in groups, conducting some preliminary experiments to determine whether or not a given variable affects the period.

"How would you judge a group member's contribution?"

Mention that you will be observing their group work the rest of today and tomorrow, focusing on cooperation. With the class, create a list of criteria on which this group work should be judged. Here are some possibilities.

- Does the group divide the task up among the members?

- Does the group agree on a plan or structure for tackling the task?

- Does the group take time to ensure that everyone understands the task?

- Does the group use its time in a productive way?

- Does the group support each member?

- Does the group record its results carefully?

Post this list of "criteria for a successful group" for students to refer to. You will probably need to keep a written record of your observations as you move from group to group.

Note: In *Homework 18: Pendulum Conclusions,* students will assign grades to themselves and to their group members based on the quality of their group work. You may want to mention this now.

5. *Initial Experiments*
(see facing page)

Either assign or let each group choose a variable from the list generated earlier. (You may need to limit their choices to be sure that at least one group looks at each of the key variables of weight, length, and amplitude.) Tell students that their goal is to determine whether the variable they are using affects the period of a pendulum.

You should provide an assortment of materials for students to use in these experiments, in addition to the standard experiment materials. The idea is for students to make their own choices, rather than for you to structure the experiments for them. There is no particular set of materials that you need; this collection can include whatever you have readily available.

As students work, remind them to keep a record of the data they collect and to write a summary of their group's work on chart paper. They should try to provide strong evidence for any conclusions they make.

Encourage groups to explore other variables if they have time.

Note: The experiments that students will do today and tomorrow are not intended to produce definitive results. Thus, you do not need to tell students how to conduct their experiment and you can let them make mistakes. These experiments should offer them some understanding of experimentation and help them with their revised experiments later in the unit.

On Days 16, 17, and 24 they will be performing other pendulum experiments with (we hope) a more sophisticated perspective.

Also, the idea of a *controlled experiment* will be explored in connection with tomorrow's discussion of tonight's homework, so you don't need to discuss this topic now.

Initial Experiments

You know that *something* determines the period of a pendulum, but it may not be clear to you exactly what that something is. Maybe there are several things.

In this activity, you will do some preliminary experiments to get an idea about what affects a pendulum's period.

1. Your teacher will assign you a variable from the list made in class. Do some experiments to see if that variable affects the period of a pendulum.

2. Prepare a written report, describing what you did, what observations you made, and what questions you still have.

Interactive Mathematics Program   315

Homework 2

Close to the Law

Zoe was doing a report on crime. Some people she interviewed believed that building more police stations would result in less crime. These people claimed that the closer one gets to a police station, the less crime there is.

Others thought that nearness to a police station was not an important factor in the level of crime in a neighborhood.

Zoe wanted to check out these competing claims. She called her local police station and got data on crimes in her area in the past year. She focused on robberies and how far each of the robberies had been from the station. She made this chart.

Number of Blocks from Police Station	Number of Crimes per Block
0–5	13
5–10	14
More than 10	16

1. Given this information, what relationship do you think there is between nearness to a police station and amount of crime? Explain your reasoning.

2. Zoe's brother Max thinks there might be other factors affecting crime rate besides distance from the police station. List at least three other factors that might account for the differences in crime rates in the table.

Homework 2: Close to the Law

The purpose of this homework is to highlight the need for identifying any possible variables that might affect the outcome of an experiment. As the unit develops, students will be looking at the issue of how to do controlled experiments in order to study the effect of a single variable.

Experiment Conclusions

Mathematical Topics

* The concept of **controlled experiment**
* Analysis of preliminary experiments

Outline of the Day

In Class

1. Discuss *Homework 2: Close to the Law*

   * Introduce the idea of a controlled experiment

2. Students finish work on *Initial Experiments* (from Day 2)

3. Discuss *Initial Experiments*

   * Ask students how confident they are that a given variable affects the period of a pendulum

At Home

Homework 3: If I Could Do It Over Again

Special Materials Needed

* Experiment materials

1. Discussion of Homework 2: Close to the Law

"What relationship do you think there is?"

Let students share their ideas on the homework situation as a whole class.

On Question 1, some students probably will think that the data support the position that having more police stations would reduce crime. According to the chart, the number of crimes does go up as the distance from the police station increases. Others may be skeptical about this conclusion. You can use their skepticism to explore why one might *not* conclude that building more police stations will decrease crime.

If no one raises the issue of the size of the differences in the table, you can ask: "What if the numbers in the table were 13, 13.1, and 13.2? Would you reach the same conclusion?"

An important issue is whether the differences shown in the table are big enough to justify any conclusions. This question will be important later in the unit, so look for opportunities to discuss it during student comments. If it doesn't come up on its own, you might ask something like "What if the numbers in the table were 13, 13.1, and 13.2? Would you reach the same conclusion?"

This discussion may blend into Question 2. Some other explanations for differences in crime rate might include lack of street lights, presence of activities that attract crime, and a higher concentration of people.

• Controlling variables

The discussion so far should have brought out that the increase shown in the table might be the result of factors other than distance from the police station.

"How might you test whether distance from the police station is the reason for the increase in crimes per block?"

Building on that idea, ask how one could determine whether the increase in crimes per block is really caused by increased distance from the police station. Students might suggest, for example, comparing blocks that are essentially the same in other ways that might affect crime, or they might suggest the need to gather data over a long period of time.

Introduce the term **controlled study** or **controlled experiment** to refer to what they are describing. See if students can put this general idea into words. They might describe it as a study or experiment in which everything is the same except the variable that is being tested.

This is students' first exposure in the IMP curriculum to the idea of a controlled experiment, so their ideas may be tentative. Students will have more experiences with controlled experiments in the next unit, *Shadows*.

2. Continued Work on *Initial Experiments*

Ask groups to continue their work from yesterday. They will of course vary in their efficiency at completing their experiments and reaching conclusions, so be sure to let all groups have enough time to compile some results.

Emphasize that each group will report the results of its experiments *at the end of the class period*. Reports should contain a conclusion *and* evidence for the conclusion.

Remind students that you will continue to assess their group work. You may wish to point out the list of "criteria for a successful group" posted on Day 2.

3. Discussion of *Initial Experiments*

Ask the heart card member of each group to report on the group's experiments.

You can follow up here on the earlier discussion of controlled experiments, which will be an important concept in later work of the unit. Thus, whenever possible, point out the difficulty in making a decision about "what matters" without keeping all variables constant except the one being studied.

Some groups may have done fairly controlled experiments, changing just one variable. They may state, for example, that they changed the weight of the bob and got a different period.

"How certain are you that your variable affects the period?"

"Did you ever get different periods for the same pendulum?"

You can ask such groups about their confidence in their results, with questions like "How certain are you that weight makes a difference? Are you 90% sure? Absolutely certain? Not certain at all?"

If the opportunity arises, ask if the groups ever measured the period of the exact same pendulum more than once and, if so, whether they got the exact same result. This issue can provide a very preliminary introduction to the idea of measurement variation. That topic will be continued in tomorrow's activity, so you needn't pursue it today if it doesn't come up naturally.

Tell students that these initial experiments are not the last ones they will perform. However, before the groups conduct additional experiments, they need to study more about how to tell whether a variable "makes a difference" to the period of a pendulum.

Lindsay Crawford is setting up her group's initial pendulum experiment.

Homework 3

If I Could Do It Over Again

The process of experimentation often requires a person to test, refine the experiment, and then test again.

Even if an experiment does not yield the expected results, important knowledge often emerges from it, such as information about what not to do.

What advice would you give someone who is doing your group's pendulum experiment for the first time? Address these issues.

- Problems encountered in setting up the experiment

- Problems encountered in doing the experiment

- Materials you would have liked to have

- Unexpected results

Homework 3: If I Could Do It Over Again

This homework asks students to reflect on their experiments of the last two days.

Problems with Measurement

Students are introduced to the concept of measurement variation.

Mathematical Topics

- Introduction to measurement variation
- Frequency bar graphs

Outline of the Day

In Class

1. Discuss *Homework 3: If I Could Do It Over Again*
2. Pose the question of whether measuring the same phenomenon will always give the same result
3. *Time Is Relative*
   - Students try to make a stopwatch stop at exactly five seconds

4. Discuss *Time Is Relative*
   - Make and post a frequency bar graph of results
   - Introduce the concept of measurement variation and add this idea to the general outline for the unit

At Home

Homework 4: What's Your Stride?

Special Materials Needed

- One stopwatch per group
- Experiment results from Days 2 and 3

Discuss With Your Colleagues

Measurement Variation

Although measurement variation is a key idea in this unit, it is not part of the standard secondary curriculum. You and your colleagues may want to support one another by discussing what it is and how it fits into the unit problem. Again, you might want to discuss this topic with science teachers.

1. Discussion of Homework 3: *If I Could Do It Over Again*

Let students share some ideas and lessons they learned. Remind them that they will do many more pendulum experiments in this unit, so these lessons can be put to good use.

2. Are Measurements Consistent?

Over the next few days, students will conduct experiments that will show that one can measure the exact same thing twice, using the same method, and get different answers. Students will also begin to see how this issue relates to the main unit problem. The current discussion is just a brief introduction to a topic that will be followed up on later today and referred to again over the next several days.

"Will all the measurements be the same?"

As an introduction to today's activity, *Time Is Relative*, pose the following question to the whole class.

> *In the most perfect pendulum experiment, do you think there would be any variation in the results? In other words, if a person timed the same pendulum over and over, would the results of measuring the period always be the same?*

Let students discuss this topic very briefly, and tell them that they will come back to it after today's activity, *Time Is Relative*.

3. *Time Is Relative*

(see facing page)

The activity *Time Is Relative* has three purposes:

- To show students how much variation can occur in measuring a fixed phenomenon

- To review the use of frequency bar graphs to display data

- To produce a set of data that approximates normal distribution.

Because this activity does not directly involve pendulums or the Poe story, you may want to point out that the central unit question involves the time required for 12 swings of a pendulum. Thus, *Time Is Relative* is relevant because it involves measuring time.

Students will need at least one stopwatch per group. Individual students will use the stopwatch to time five seconds on someone's wristwatch or on the

Time Is Relative

Nobody is a perfect timer. In this experiment you will explore how accurately people can time things. Members of your group will take turns timing five seconds.

Here is how the experiment works.

- One person watches the second hand of the clock on the wall or on a group member's watch. A second person holds a stopwatch.

- The first person says, "Start," and then says, "Stop" after five seconds. The second person tries to make the stopwatch start and stop on command so that it reads five seconds at the end of the experiment.

You will naturally be off a little bit each time you try it. Record your results to the nearest tenth of a second. Take turns timing and recording the results.

classroom clock. Students can take turns within their group timing five seconds to the nearest tenth of a second, recording each of their results.

Let students work on this task for about ten minutes. Then bring them together for a discussion and sharing of data.

4. Discussion of *Time Is Relative*

The next task is for students to make a frequency bar graph of their data. This graph will be one of the examples used on Day 7, when the normal distribution is introduced.

You may need to review what a frequency bar graph is and how to make one. (Students were introduced to frequency bar graphs in *The Game*

of Pig.) Essentially, they need to recall that a frequency bar graph is a graph that shows how often each particular result or range of results occurs.

Also, tomorrow is a relatively light day, so if you don't finish the discussion of *Time Is Relative* today, you can conclude it tomorrow.

• *Frequency bar graph of timing data*

Tell students that their next task is to make a frequency bar graph of their data. They can begin by finding out the spread of the data—that is, what the highest and lowest results were within the class.

"What is a good way to group the data?"

Then, on the basis of this information, have the class decide on a way to group the data. Because students were to give their results to the nearest tenth of a second, they will have to decide how many possible results to put in each grouping. Be sure students are aware that each grouping should cover an equal range of possible results.

Discuss the pros and cons of various groupings. The major point to bring out is that, if there are too many or too few subintervals, the graph won't look very interesting; that is, they won't see any patterns in the graph.

For example, students might express the groupings as "4.6 or 4.7," "4.8 or 4.9," "5.0 or 5.1," "5.2 or 5.3," and so on.

It would be somewhat misleading to express the groupings as "4.6–4.7," "4.8–4.9," "5.0–5.1," "5.2–5.3," and so

on. For example, the grouping "4.6 or 4.7" really represents any outcome between 4.55 and 4.75.

Note: Our experience is that listing each possible result individually leads to a fairly meaningful graph.

Post this graph for use in the introduction to normal distributions on Day 7.

• *Measurement variation*

After the graph is complete, make sure students realize that all of them were trying to measure exactly the same thing but they came up with a range of results. (They may be surprised at how far from five seconds some of the results are.)

*"What does
measurement
variation have
to do with the
unit problem?"*

Tell students that this phenomenon is referred to as **measurement variation**, **measurement error**, or **measurement uncertainty**.

Ask the class what measurement variation has to do with the unit problem. If they need a hint, point to step 1 of the outline created on Day 2: "Find out which variable or variables affect the period of the pendulum." (See the section "The General Plan.")

*"How does the idea
of measurement
variation affect your
conclusions from
'Initial Experiments?'"*

In particular, ask what this variation tells them about the previous two days' pendulum experiments. Bring out—pushing the idea a bit if needed—that the variations they saw among different pendulums might have been due only to measurement variation.

Ask them to take a brief look at their conclusions from those experiments, and tell them that they will conduct another set of experiments later on, when they have a fuller understanding of the issue of measurement variation.

- *A subheading in the outline: Measurement variation*

   Tell students that learning about measurement variation will take them on a major digression away from pendulums. Add a subheading, such as "measurement variation," under step 1 of the outline.

Homework 4: What's Your Stride?
(see next page)

Introduce the word *stride* to the class in preparation for this homework, and go over the way this term is defined in the assignment.

Homework 4   What's Your Stride?

Your **stride** is the length of a typical step when you are walking normally at a steady rate. For this assignment, you should measure a stride from the front of one foot to the front of the other foot.

Give all measurements to the nearest inch.

1. Take a guess at the length of your stride, and write it down.

2. Measuring your own stride may not be easy.

   a. Think of a method for measuring the length of your own stride, and describe it clearly.

   b. Use your method to find the length of your stride.

3. Using the same method, find the length of a stride of each of two people not in your class. (You can work with family members, neighbors, friends, and so on. In order to avoid too wide a variation, you should work only with people who are teenagers or older.)

4. What do you think a frequency bar graph of the stride lengths of 50 people might look like? Based on your best guess, make such a graph.

5. Why might people want to know the lengths of their strides?

Homework discussion and pulse experiments provide further insight into measurement variation.

DAY 5 *How Often?*

Mathematical Topics

• Making and interpreting frequency bar graphs

Outline of the Day

In Class

1. Select presenters for tomorrow's discussion of *POW 12: The Big Knight Switch*
2. Discuss *Homework 4: What's Your Stride?*
   • Ask students to describe different methods of measuring stride length
   • Make and post a frequency bar graph of homework data

3. *Pulse Gathering*
   • Students measure their pulses several times and compile the data for use in tonight's homework
   • No whole-class discussion of this activity is needed

At Home

Homework 5: Pulse Analysis

1. POW Presentation Preparation

Presentations of *POW 12: The Big Knight Switch* are scheduled for tomorrow. Choose three students to make POW presentations, and give them overhead transparencies and pens to take home to use in their preparations.

2. Discussion of *Homework 4: What's Your Stride?*

Note: As in their work on *Homework 1: Building a Pendulum,* students may have used different methods to measure the length of a single stride (such as measuring the total length of several strides and dividing by the number of strides). When they do their experiments for *The Standard Pendulum* on Day 16, students will need to have a uniform measurement procedure. You may want to explain very briefly that the first part of the homework discussion below anticipates work later in the unit.

- ## *Methods of measurement*

    Ask students to work in groups to do the following tasks.

    - List all the different methods for calculating stride length that their group came up with

    - Discuss the strengths and weaknesses of each method of calculation

    After each group has had time to list the methods and discuss them, ask the spade card member of each group to report. As students list new ways of measuring stride, write the methods on the chart paper.

- ## *Frequency bar graph of stride data*

    The next part of the homework discussion is for the class to prepare a frequency bar graph (on chart paper so it can be saved) showing the stride lengths for the students in the class.

    "How do you want to group the data?"

    In order to make the graph, the class will have to decide on intervals in which to group the data. You may want to suggest that, as a first step, they find out the high and low values of the results. Also, bring out again, if needed, that it is important that the intervals be of equal width; otherwise, the graph will give a misleading picture of the results.

    For example, if measurements are given to the nearest inch, the graph might include bars representing

    - the number of students with stride from 30 to 34 inches

    - the number of students with stride from 35 to 39 inches

    - the number of students with stride from 40 to 44 inches

    and so on.

    Ask each group to total the number of results they have in each interval. Combine these group totals and make the graph.

    Post the graph for use in the introduction to normal distributions on Day 7.

    If time allows, make more than one version of the frequency bar graph, using a different choice for the width of the intervals, and compare the results. You may want to combine the data from different classes. In this case, the data from each class should be entered in a different color on the graph so that students can see their own results.

• *Question 5*

"Why would you want to know the length of your stride?"

As time permits, let students share their ideas about why one might want to know the length of one's stride.

3. *Pulse Gathering*

(see next page)

Have students read *Pulse Gathering*. Make sure all of them can find their pulses on their own wrists. Caution them against feeling for their pulse with their thumb, because thumbs have a pulse of their own. Tell them that they will be working with the data from *Pulse Gathering* in tonight's homework.

You should combine groups, if needed, so that each student has data for at least two other students.

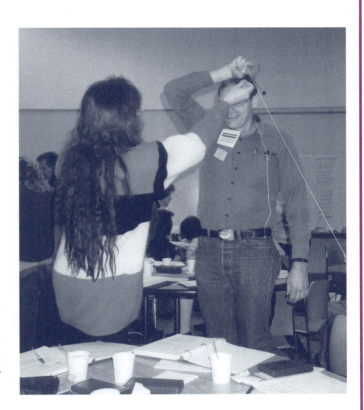

During a teacher inservice, George Giffen assists an IMP colleague in determining whether amplitude matters.

Pulse Gathering

If you repeatedly measure the same thing very carefully in the same way, will you get the same answer every time?

This activity provides a setting in which to look at this question.

1. Begin with your body at rest. Then count the pulse beats at your wrist for a 15-second interval. Record your result as a whole number of pulse beats.

2. Repeat step 1, again recording your result. Continue to repeat step 1 until you have ten results. (Some of these results may be identical.)

3. In preparation for *Homework 5: Pulse Analysis,* share your data with everyone else in your group, and record each other's results. In other words, you should have ten results for each person in the group (including yourself).

The Pit and the Pendulum

Homework

Homework 5 Pulse Analysis

You should have a collection of data on the number of pulse beats in a 15-second interval—ten results for yourself and ten for each of your fellow group members.

1. Did you get the same result each time you counted your pulse beats for a 15-second interval? Why or why not?

2. a. Find the mean (average) of your own pulse data.

   b. Find the mean of the pulse data for your whole group.

   c. Was the whole group's mean the same as your own? Why or why not?

3. For the following frequency bar graphs, do not group your measurements.

   a. Make a frequency bar graph of your own pulse data.

   b. Make a frequency bar graph for the pulse data of the whole group.

Homework 5: Pulse Analysis

In this assignment, students will do some analysis of the data from the activity *Pulse Gathering*.

POW 12 Presentations

Students present POW 12 and also make frequency bar graphs from their pulse experiment results.

Mathematical Topics

- Record keeping as part of problem solving
- Continued work with measurement variation and frequency bar graphs

Outline of the Day

In Class

1. Presentations of *POW 12: The Big Knight Switch*
2. Discuss *Homework 5: Pulse Analysis*
   - Continue to develop the concept of measurement variation
   - Examine variation from one individual to another
   - Make and post a frequency bar graph of the data

At Home

Homework 6: Return to the Pit

POW 13: Corey Camel (due Day 14)

   - Students will get a mini-POW related to this on Day 8

1. Presentations of *POW 12: The Big Knight Switch*

"Did anyone switch the knights in fewer moves?"

"How did you keep track of the moves?"

Ask the three students to make their POW presentations. If other students were able to move the knights in fewer moves, let them share their methods. (The best answer to this problem is 16.)

Ask students to discuss their different methods of keeping track of moves so that they did not double-count. Also, ask them to discuss why they feel they cannot do the task in fewer moves. They probably won't have complete proofs here, but this is a good opportunity for them to work on developing convincing arguments.

Note: Two supplemental problems, *More Knights Switching* and *A Knight Goes Traveling,* are available for students who want to do more of this type of analysis.

2. Discussion of *Homework 5: Pulse Analysis*

"Did you get the same pulse rate each time you measured?"

Ask students whether they got the same pulse rate each time they measured. (They almost certainly did not.) Discuss why they did not. Bring out that the variation could have been due either to an actual change in pulse rate or to measurement variation.

Use this assignment as an occasion to clarify once again the concept of measurement variation. You may want to have students think back to their work on *Time Is Relative* (Day 4).

"What role does measurement variation play in the unit problem?"

Again, ask about the role of this phenomenon in the unit problem. Students should be realizing that measurement variation will be crucial as they try to determine whether a variable affects the period of a pendulum swing. In doing their experiments to measure the period of a pendulum, they will need to decide whether a change in measurement is due to measurement variation or to the effect of a change in a variable. To make this decision wisely, they will need to understand measurement variation.

IMP teacher Dwight Fuller measures the amplitude of his group's pendulum.

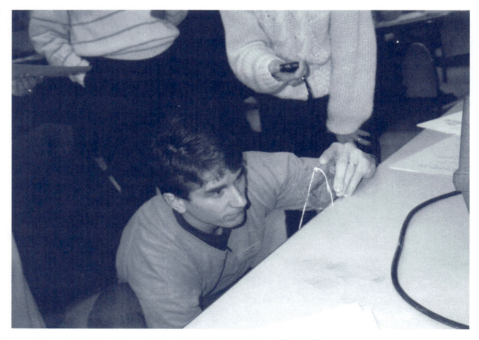

- *Variations from one individual to another*

Ask students how much the data varied from person to person, and why. You need not get into biology issues here, but the discussion should bring out that different people may have different pulse rates at rest.

"Can you tell from one measurement whose pulse it was?"

Ask whether they could tell from a single measurement in their list which person the pulse rate came from. Even though different individuals probably had different means, there was most likely some overlap in results. For example, one person may have had measurements between 16 and 20, and another may have had measurements from 18 to 22. The point to bring out is that a measurement of, say, 19 could have come from either person. Taking one measurement from each person wouldn't necessarily tell you which person had the higher mean pulse rate.

- *Frequency bar graphs of pulse data*

You can ask students if they made any observations about how their group graphs (from Question 3b) compared to their individual graphs (from Question 3a). (If they have no comments to make, you can just move on.)

Then compile a master chart of pulse rates using the data from the entire class. Each group should already have subtotals (from making the graphs for Question 3b), which you can use to get the totals for the whole class. (In a class of 30 students, there will be 300 individual data items.)

You may want to discuss the spread of the data. If any results are very far afield, ask for possible explanations.

Then ask each group to put the data into a frequency bar graph, as was done with the timing and stride data. Let groups make their own decisions about possible ways to group the data. If time allows, students can make one graph on which data items are grouped and another on which they are not.

You can either post several of these graphs or choose one and post it as representative. The graph(s) will be used in the introduction to normal distributions on Day 7.

Homework 6: Return to the Pit
(see next page)

This assignment asks students to summarize where they are in the process of solving the unit problem and, specifically, to reflect on the role of measurement variation.

Homework 6   Return to the Pit

This unit is complex and includes some investigations that are not directly concerned with the main problem.

Therefore, from time to time in this unit, we will ask you to reflect on where you are with respect to solving the unit problem.

Write answers to these questions so that someone who knows nothing about the story and knows little about mathematics could understand what you are saying.

1. Write about the problem that the class is trying to solve, stating the goal as clearly as you can.

2. Write about what you have done so far in the unit and how that work will help to solve the unit problem. Be sure to explain clearly how measurement variation is involved.

3. Finally, write down some questions you have about the unit and some points you don't yet clearly understand.

322   Interactive Mathematics Program

POW 13   Corey Camel

Consider the case of Corey Camel—the enterprising but eccentric owner of a small banana grove in a remote desert oasis.

Corey's harvest, which is worth its weight in gold, consists of 3000 bananas. The marketplace where the harvest can be sold is 1000 miles away. However, Corey must walk to the market, and she can carry at most 1000 bananas at a time. Furthermore, being a camel, Corey eats one banana during each and every mile she walks (so Corey can never walk anywhere without bananas).

The question is this:

How many bananas can Corey get to the market?

Write-up

1. *Problem statement*

2. *Process:* You will also work on a mini-POW that relates to this POW. In discussing your process on this POW, note how your work on that mini-POW helped you. Also, be sure to discuss all of the methods you tried in order to solve the POW itself.

3. *Solution:*

   a. State your solution (or solutions) as clearly as you can.

   b. Do you think your solution is the best possible one? Explain.

   c. Explain how and why the answer to this POW is related to the answer to the mini-POW.

4. *Evaluation*

POW 13: Corey Camel

This POW will probably be difficult for students, and they will work on a simpler version (*A Mini-POW About Mini-Camel*) on Day 8. (You should mention that later activity now, because the write-up instructions refer to it.) Students will then come back to this original version and try to apply their insights. This POW is scheduled to be presented on Day 14.

Statistics and the Pendulum

This page in the student book introduces Days 7 through 15.

So now you've got an idea of what this unit problem is all about. You probably have a list of variables that might affect the period of a pendulum, but you've also seen that you can measure the exact same pendulum twice and get different periods. That makes things pretty unpredictable!

Actually, scientists are used to uncertainty in their experiments. You might say that this uncertainty is "normal." In the part of mathematics called statistics, people have a very special meaning for the word *normal,* and they've come up with ways to describe how *abnormal* a particular measurement might be.

Lindsey Carvalho prepares a bar graph as an aid in analyzing the results from her experiment.

What's Normal?

> *The concept of normal distribution is introduced.*

Mathematical Topics

- Bell-shaped curves and normal distributions
- Symmetry and concavity and their relationship to the normal curve

Outline of the Day

In Class

1. Discuss *Homework 6: Return to the Pit*
2. Introduce the concept of the **normal distribution**
   - Describe the normal distribution as a special bell-shaped curve
   - Bring out that the curve has a line of symmetry at the mean
   - Point out the change in concavity

- Introduce and post the "Normality Assumption" about pendulum data
- Add the concept of normal distribution to the general outline of the unit

At Home

Homework 7: What's Normal?

Special Materials Needed

- Frequency bar graphs (from Days 4–6) on the timing of five seconds, on students' strides, and on students' pulse rates
- Overhead transparencies of normal curves (see Appendix B)

Discuss With Your Colleagues

What If You Never Studied Statistics?

The normal distribution and standard deviation, as well as the application of these ideas in the unit, will be new to most secondary teachers. Generally, teachers report that after teaching this unit once or twice, they are very comfortable with the ideas. Most instructors, however, do need support their first time through.

It will be helpful if you can articulate your understandings of how these ideas fit into the solution of the unit problem. You might also benefit from sharing your uneasiness about working with students in an area where you may feel shaky.

1. Discussion of *Homework 6: Return to the Pit*

Ask a few volunteers to share their views of what the problem is and how the work so far fits into its solution. Try to get students to state clearly where they are headed and what role measurement variation plays.

List students' questions on the overhead, and see whether other students can answer them. Use as much or as little time as you think is needed to clarify issues.

2. The Normal Distribution

Later in the unit, the ideas of normal distribution and standard deviation will play a critical role in determining what factors affect the period of a pendulum. Today's work introduces students to the normal distribution.

Draw students' attention to the frequency bar graphs made earlier. Three graphs should have been posted.

- Timing of five seconds (made on Day 4, from *Time Is Relative*)

- Students' strides (made on Day 5, from *Homework 4: What's Your Stride?*)

- Students' pulse rates (made on Day 6, from *Homework 5: Pulse Analysis*)

Celeste Bookwalter, Brenna Borelli, Jody Dunham, and Alex Wellerstein make friends with standard deviation (see activity on Day 13).

Ask students to comment on the general shape of the graphs. Ask them what features the graphs share. They will probably focus on two key features.

- The graphs are highest "in the middle." (Students may or may not use the term *mean*.)

- The graphs gradually go down toward both ends.

Show students the curve below, and tell them that curves with this general appearance are called **bell shaped**. Mention that there is a very special bell-shaped curve called the **normal distribution**. (The following diagram and the three others in today's notes are provided separately in Appendix B for use in making overhead transparencies.)

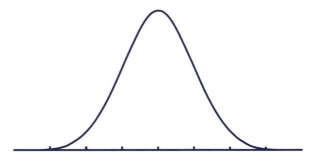

When a curve is used to describe data distribution, the general idea is that the area under a given part of the curve represents the portion of measurements that fall within the given values. Students should see the similarity between this area and the area of a bar in a frequency bar graph.

For example, if the shaded area on the next diagram is, say, 20% of the total area under the curve, then 20% of all measurements are between a and b.

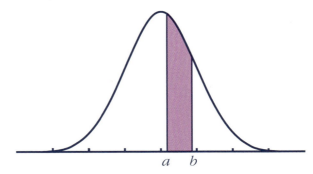

You can also show students the next diagram, which depicts three different normal curves on the same set of axes. Explain that the amount of variation from one measurement to another is different in different situations, and that the exact shape of a normal curve depends on the scales being used and the specific situation.

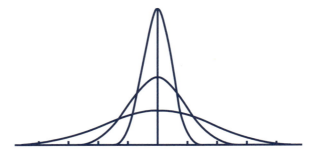

As indicated earlier, the normal distribution is a very specific type of bell-shaped frequency pattern, with a precise, technical mathematical definition. It is useful in many statistical situations, not just in studying measurement variation.

Tell students that we are giving them only an intuitive description of the normal distribution. Therefore, they will not be able to determine for sure if something is or is not normally distributed. The precise definition involves a complex formula for the graph—one that most people see only if they study statistics in college. Tell students that this complex formula is part of a Year 4 unit called *The Pollster's Dilemma,* in which they will learn much more about how normal distributions can be used.

• *Technical versus everyday use of the word "normal"*

You may want to clarify that in the term *normal distribution,* the word *normal* is being used in a very special, technical sense. It does not mean "ordinary," although the normal distribution is one that occurs commonly in many situations.

• *The line of symmetry and the mean*

"What features do the normal curves have in common?"

Ask for comments about the general shape of these normal curves.

Students should see that, as with the frequency bar graphs under consideration today, the normal curve graphs are highest in the middle and decrease gradually toward both ends. But students should observe one more specific phenomenon:

The normal curve is symmetric.

(Give hints or point this out yourself if students don't see it.)

Introduce the term **line of symmetry** for the vertical line that divides the graph into two equal parts.

"What does the symmetry of the graph tell you about where the mean is?"

Ask students what this symmetry tells them about where the mean should be. They should realize that values to the right of the line of symmetry will balance out with values to the left of that line. Help them as needed to use this observation to reach an important conclusion:

The mean is exactly at the line of symmetry.

• *Concavity in the normal curve*

Another subtle observation on the shape of the graph concerns **concavity**.

"How does the normal curve change the way it 'curves'?"

You can bring this out by asking if students see any change in the way the graph "curves." Use an overhead transparency of the diagram below to illustrate the ideas if students don't suggest them. Introduce the terms **concave up** and **concave down** to describe the different portions of the curve as shown in the diagram.

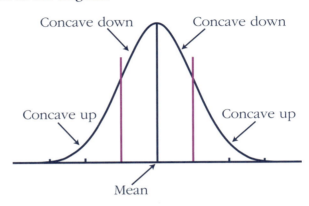

You may want to describe a curve that is concave up as "holding water" and a curve that is concave down as "shedding water."

Although this may seem like a minor issue, the change of concavity plays an important role in providing a visual image of standard deviation.

The significance of concavity in relation to standard deviation will be discussed on Day 13.

• *Normal distribution and measurement data*

"Do you think the graphs of your experiment data resemble the normal distribution?"

Ask students if they think their graphs of strides, timing, or pulses resemble the normal distribution. Their response may depend on how much data they collected for each experiment and on the way they grouped results.

Whatever their response, tell them that if they recorded more and more data, their graphs would probably begin to look more and more like the normal distribution. The normal curve is generally considered a reasonable expectation for results of measurement variation.

Tell them that, based on this general experiment phenomenon, this unit makes the following assumption:

Normality Assumption

> If you make many measurements of the period of any given pendulum, the data will closely fit a normal distribution.

You should post this assumption, since it will be used later in the unit.

If it seems appropriate to your class, you might describe the normal graph intuitively as the result of making the intervals from the bar graph narrower and narrower and of using more and more data.

Again, you may want to remind students that this is only an informal description of the normal distribution.

• *Another subheading in the outline: Normal distribution*

"How does the idea of normal distribution relate to the unit problem?"

Ask students how the idea of normal distribution is connected with the unit problem. Refer them, if necessary, to the outline from Day 2. This outline should already include a subheading such as "measurement variation" (see Day 4).

Students should recognize that, according to the "normality assumption," the normal distribution describes the kind of measurement variation that they should expect in pendulum experiments. Therefore, familiarity with the normal distribution is moving them along in the process of determining which variables are important.

Add something like "normal distribution" as a further subheading under "measurement variation."

> • *Note for teachers: Two contexts for the normal distribution*
>
> The earlier examples illustrate two different types of situations in which the normal distribution is likely to be appropriate.
>
> • Distribution of many instances of a given phenomenon, measured across a population (for example, the strides of the different students in the class).
>
> • Distribution of many measurements of the same instance of a given phenomenon (for example, timing five seconds over and over).
>
> The distinction between these two categories isn't always clear. For example, is measuring your own pulse rate many times an example of the first type or the second type? Use your judgment about whether or not to mention this distinction to students. In any case, don't worry about making the distinction absolutely clear to them.

• •

We used dry erase markers to draw normal distribution curves on the windows. They've been there for a year and have been a great point of reference during [the Year 2 unit] "Is There Really a Difference?".

IMP Teacher Mike Christensen

Homework 7   What's Normal?

You've now seen some examples of normal curves. But when does the normal distribution apply to real life?

This assignment describes several situations. You may not know what the real information is, so just do your best. You might just make up a set of data that seems reasonable to you.

For each situation, follow these steps.

a. Draw a frequency bar graph of the situation based on your idea of what the data might look like. Your graph should show labeled axes and units of measurement, and you will need to decide on intervals that are suitable to the situation.

b. Explain how you decided what the graph should look like. If you guessed, explain what made you guess the way you did.

c. State whether or not your graph appears to be approximately a normal distribution.

1. The number of people in your school who wear hightop tennis shoes, lowtop tennis shoes, dress shoes, or sandals to school on a given day.

2. The frequency with which a 100-meter sprinter achieves certain times, running 200 races over the course of one year. (Assume that the sprinter's average time is 12 seconds.)

3. The number of people in the United States who earn certain amounts of money. (Use 250,000,000 as the total population of the United States. You might use categories such as "income from $0 to $20,000," "income from $20,000 to $40,000," "income from $40,000 to $60,000," and so on.)

4. The number of people in the state of Hawaii who are of certain ages. (Use 1,100,000 as the total population of Hawaii.)

Homework 7: What's Normal?

Point out to students that this assignment asks them to create graphs involving labeled axes and units of measurement. They will need to decide on the intervals and estimate the amounts in each interval.

Mini-POW About Mini-Camel

Students work on a simpler version of their POW.

Mathematical Topics

- Characterizing data as normally distributed or not
- Solving problems using trial and error
- Using manipulatives in problem solving

Outline of the Day

In Class

1. Discuss *Homework 7: What's Normal?*
2. *A Mini-POW About Mini-Camel*
   - Students look at a simpler version of the POW
3. Discuss *A Mini-POW About Mini-Camel*
   - Students present their results

- If no one has the optimal solution, leave it as an open question

At Home

Homework 8: Flip, Flip

1. Discussion of *Homework 7: What's Normal?*

"Which situations do you think are normally distributed?"

Have students compare, in groups, the graphs they sketched. The class as a whole can then discuss which situations they think are normally distributed.

On Question 1, some students may have arranged the categories so that the tallest frequency bars are in the middle and then concluded that the distribution is approximately normal. If so, point out that a normal distribution requires that the data items be numerical in nature. The categories for types of shoes are not numerical.

Of Questions 2 through 4, only the situation in Question 2 might be approximately normally distributed (and even that might not be), although students may not have the facts on which to make this judgment.

For Question 3, you can tell students that far more people have incomes below the mean than above it (due to the effect on the mean of a small number of people with very high incomes). Income distribution does resemble the normal distribution in at least one respect: It trails off toward the extremes (at least at the upper end).

For Question 4, help students to see that, assuming either constant or increasing birthrates, the population of different age groups decreases gradually toward the higher age groups. For example, there are generally more people between the ages of 0 and 10 than between 10 and 20, more between 10 and 20 than between 20 and 30, and so on.

However, Hawaii could be an exception to this pattern, because it attracts a large number of retired people.

You can tell students that many properties of people and objects are distributed normally or close to normally, but many are not. It isn't necessarily easy to decide in theory which are which.

Review the assumption that is being made in this unit—that measurements of a given pendulum's period are normally distributed.

2. *A Mini-POW About Mini-Camel*
(see facing page)

"How is work progressing on the POW?"

Ask students how their work is going on *POW 13: Corey Camel.* They are probably finding it difficult. Ask them to work in groups (or in pairs) on the following simplified version of their POW.

Pass out beans for each group (at least 45 beans for each pair).

Any students who have already solved the POW can be asked to give hints to their groups about how to solve *A Mini-POW About Mini-Camel.* Emphasize that they should not tell the group the solution, but just give subtle suggestions regarding types of things to think about.

Urge students to keep notes on how they solve this problem, since their notes should help them on the POW itself.

3. Discussion of *A Mini-POW About Mini-Camel*

"What helps to make an explanation clear?"

Ask two or three members of the class to present their solutions to the mini-POW. Discuss features that help make explanations clear. You might delay a discussion of how the mini-POW relates to the POW.

A Mini-POW About Mini-Camel

Like Corey Camel, Mini-Camel also owns a banana grove.

But Mini-Camel's harvest consists of only 45 bananas, and Mini-Camel can carry at most 15 bananas at a time.

The marketplace where Mini-Camel's harvest can be sold is only 15 miles away. Like Corey, however, Mini-Camel also eats one banana during each and every mile he walks.

1. How many bananas can Mini-Camel get to market?

2. Explain how Mini-Camel achieves this result.

3. Discuss how the Mini-Camel problem is related to *POW 13: Corey Camel,* and explain how the mini-POW could help you solve the POW.

Note: Your POW write-up asks you to refer to your work on this assignment, so you'll need to keep a copy of your notes from this mini-POW.

326

Note: The best possible result for Mini-Camel is to get eight bananas to market. If no one has gotten a result this good, tell students that there is a better answer than they have found, but don't tell them what it is or how to get it.

Homework 8:
Flip, Flip
(see facing page)

This homework will illustrate to students that experimental data may differ from what is expected. You may want to emphasize again the importance of gathering genuine data on this and similar assignments.

It may help to let students get started on this assignment in class. You can demonstrate that a single experiment consists of flipping the entire bunch of coins and counting the number of heads. (If students don't have ten coins available, they can flip one coin ten times or do another variation, but that will take longer.)

***IMP teachers
Julie Goldstein and
George Martinez
work together during
an inservice.***

Homework 8

Flip, Flip

Do the results of coin flips give a bell-shaped distribution? You can get an idea by performing some experiments.

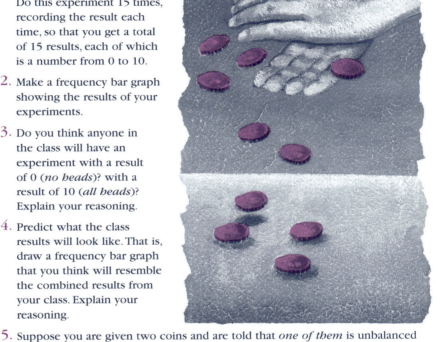

1. Shake 10 coins together and let them fall, and then record the number of heads. Do this experiment 15 times, recording the result each time, so that you get a total of 15 results, each of which is a number from 0 to 10.

2. Make a frequency bar graph showing the results of your experiments.

3. Do you think anyone in the class will have an experiment with a result of 0 (*no heads*)? with a result of 10 (*all heads*)? Explain your reasoning.

4. Predict what the class results will look like. That is, draw a frequency bar graph that you think will resemble the combined results from your class. Explain your reasoning.

5. Suppose you are given two coins and are told that *one of them* is unbalanced (but you don't know which one). You flip one of the coins 50 times, and it gives 28 heads and 22 tails. How confident would you be in deciding whether or not the coin you flipped is the unbalanced one? Explain your reasoning.

DAY 9

What's Rare?

Students use earlier data to examine "ordinary" and "rare."

Mathematical Topics

- Variation in coin-flip experiments
- Increased understanding of measurement variation
- Characterizing of data as *ordinary* or *rare*

Outline of the Day

In Class

1. Discuss *Homework 8: Flip, Flip*
   - Bring out that coin-flip results do not match the theoretical probabilities
2. *What's Rare?*
   - Students characterize various experimental results as "ordinary" or "rare"

3. Discuss *What's Rare?*
   - Suggest the need to develop a numerical method for characterizing results as "ordinary" or "rare"

At Home

Homework 9: Penny Weight

Special Materials Needed

- Frequency bar graphs (from Days 4–6) on the timing of five seconds, on students' strides, and on students' pulse rates

1. Discussion of *Homework 8: Flip, Flip*

"What does your frequency bar graph look like?"

Ask students to give verbal descriptions of their frequency bar graphs from the homework. They will probably indicate that most results are "in the middle" with fewer results at the extremes; the descriptions may not be more detailed than that.

Have each group total the number of times each possible result occurred among its members (that is, how many 0's, how many 1's, and so on). Then have group representatives read the totals out loud so that a master total can be produced on the board.

It may be interesting to see whether any 0's (no heads) or 10's (all heads) occurred, as well as what the students' expectations were.

Interactive Mathematics Program

57

Note: In a class of 30 students, the probability is about 36% that at least one person will get a 0, about 36% that at least one person will get a 10, and about 59% that at least one of these two extreme cases will occur.

For Question 4, students are likely to think that the graph will look normal. In fact, the theoretical distribution of the coin flips is quite close to normal.

The most important element of the homework assignment at this point is Question 5, because the goal is to develop some sense of what conclusions to draw from unusual results. Ask students to discuss how much *deviation* (use the word) you would have to see in order to decide that the coin was really different.

In particular, if anyone got an experiment result of 0 or 10 (or even 1 or 9), you can ask if that person concluded that the coins he or she used were unbalanced.

Students should be realizing that they should generally expect some deviation from the average. They should also be gradually developing some intuition about what level of deviation should be regarded as significant.

The coin-flip distribution will be studied in detail in the third-year unit *Pennant Fever*, and will also be studied in the fourth-year unit *The Pollster's Dilemma*. Therefore, you do not need to discuss the distribution here. It is enough that you confirm students' belief that the distribution is approximately normal.

2. *What's Rare?*
(see facing page)

The next activity, *What's Rare?,* asks students to make decisions based on the frequency bar graphs that were made for pulse rate, stride length, and the timing of five seconds. (These frequency bar graphs should already be posted where everyone can see them.)

The purpose of this activity is to help students develop an intuition about what is ordinary and what is rare—an intuition that will form the basis for the concept of standard deviation. This concept, in turn, will play a key role in helping students decide what factors affect the period of a pendulum.

Comment: The two categories of ordinary and rare need not cover all possibilities. Your students may decide that some results fall between the two.

Tell students that any member may be chosen to report for the group, so each group member should record the group's decisions and reasoning.

What's Rare?

Part I: Stride Lengths

Use the frequency bar graph of stride lengths to answer these questions.

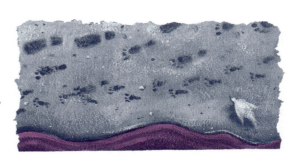

1. Name a single stride length that you would categorize as *ordinary*, and name a single stride length that you would categorize as *rare*.

2. Where would you put the boundaries for each category? In other words, complete these sentences.

    a. An ordinary stride length is from –?– to –?–.

    b. A rare stride length is less than –?– or greater than –?–.

3. Based on your answers to Question 2, estimate the answer to the following questions.

    a. What percentage of all the data is in the "ordinary" category?

    b. What percentage of all the data is in the "rare" category?

Part II: Pulse Rates

Use the frequency bar graph of pulse rates to categorize these measurements as ordinary or rare for the pulse rate of a person at rest.

1. 20 beats for 15 seconds

2. 17 beats for 15 seconds

3. 12 beats for 15 seconds

4. 28 beats for 15 seconds

Continued on next page

3. Discussion of
   What's Rare?

You might want to use a deck of cards to decide which suit of each group reports. Choose a new card for each group, so that different suits report.

5. Where would you place the borderline for each of the categories, ordinary and rare?

   a. An ordinary pulse rate is from –?– to –?–.

   b. A rare pulse rate is less than –?– or greater than –?–.

6. Based on your answers to Question 5, estimate the answers to the following questions.

   a. What percentage of all the data is in the "ordinary" category?

   b. What percentage of all the data is in the "rare" category?

Part III: Timing of Five Seconds

Use the frequency bar graph of the timing of five seconds to answer these questions.

1. Where would you place the borderline for each of the categories, ordinary and rare?

   a. An ordinary result is from –?– to –?–.

   b. A rare result is less than –?– or greater than –?–.

2. Based on your answers to Question 1, estimate the answers to the following questions.

   a. What percentage of all the data is in the "ordinary" category?

   b. What percentage of all the data is in the "rare" category?

Part IV: Comparing and Using Rarities

1. Compare the percentages you got in Question 2 of Part III with those you chose in Question 3 of Part I and Question 6 of Part II.

2. Suppose you got a new stopwatch, and used it to repeat the "timing of five seconds" experiments. If you found that you had an average of 5.7 seconds after 10 timings, would you think the new stopwatch was defective? What if your average after 10 timings with the new stopwatch was 4.9 seconds? Explain your reasoning.

"How did you decide what to call 'ordinary' and what to call 'rare'?"

"How did you decide on the percentages?"

The distinction between ordinary and rare is an arbitrary one. However, it should be interesting to have groups share how they decided to define these terms and what percentages were associated with each.

"Were your percentages the same for all three situations?"

Discuss whether the percentages defining ordinary and rare for one set of data hold up for another set of data. That is, see if there is some consistency from situation to situation in what students mean by these terms. (If so, you will be able to build on this result when students look at standard deviation.)

Finally, you may also want to discuss the question of whether the timing instruments or the person doing the timing was responsible for the variation in results for the "timing of five seconds" experiment.

- *Another subheading in the outline: The numerical meaning of "ordinary" and "rare"*

"How are these ideas connected to the unit problem?"

Ask students how their work of the last few days relates to the unit problem. As before, go back to the outline from Day 2, if needed. On Day 4 you should have added a subheading to step 1 such as "measurement variation," and on Day 7 you should have added another subheading such as "normal distribution."

Students should see that they have been gaining further insight into how the normal distribution works—what level of variation can be considered "ordinary" and what level can be considered "rare" in normally distributed data.

Tell them that the next stage of this process will be to learn about a tool statisticians use to quantify these levels more precisely. You should add something like the following as another subheading of step 1 of the outline:

> *Give numerical meaning to* ordinary *and* rare.

Assure students, if necessary, that they will be returning to the pendulum question.

Comment: Since direct work with pendulums is still some time away (Day 16), these returns to the outline and further amplifications are a good technique for maintaining continuity with the unit problem.

Homework 9: Penny Weight
(see next page)

This homework provides students the opportunity to use their intuition about measurement variation to make a decision.

Students will revisit the data from this assignment in *Homework 14: Penny Weight Revisited,* when they will look again at Question 2 of tonight's assignment with the tool of standard deviation in mind.

Homework 9 Penny Weight

Sarah's and Tom's mom is a chemist, and one day she brought home a very sensitive scale. Sarah and Tom enjoyed learning how to use the scale.

One of the things they did was measure the weight of some pennies, one at a time. Here is a list of the results they got, arranged from lightest to heaviest (weights are in milligrams).

2600	2604	2607	2610	2612	2615	2616
2617	2618	2619	2623	2623	2624	2625
2626	2627	2630	2631	2636	2637	

1. Given this information, what do you think is the best estimate for the weight of a penny, and why?

2. Sarah's and Tom's Uncle Jack claimed that he had a counterfeit penny. Sarah and Tom didn't believe it was counterfeit, because it looked real and felt real and because their uncle was always trying to fool them. They asked him if they could borrow the penny, and they weighed it. They got 2641 milligrams.

Tom said the coin must be counterfeit because they never got a weight that high with their other pennies. Sarah isn't sure. She thinks that if they weighed it again, its weight might be closer to that of the weight of the others. Or, if they measured more pennies, then Uncle Jack's coin might not seem so weird. What do you think, and why? If you don't think Uncle Jack's penny is counterfeit, then how heavy or light would a penny need to be before you believed it was counterfeit?

Mean School Data

Students use fictional data to begin looking at the concept of data spread.

Mathematical Topics

- Evaluating unusual data
- Introduction to the concept of **data spread**

Outline of the Day

In Class

1. Form new random groups
2. Discuss *Homework 9: Penny Weight*
   - Tell students that they will be developing a tool for the kind of decision-making required in this problem
3. *Mean School Data*
   - Students compare two data sets with the same mean

4. Discuss *Mean School Data*
   - Bring out the underlying question of whether a given result fits within the measurement variation of a given experiment

At Home

Homework 10: An (AB)Normal Rug

1. Forming New Groups

This is an excellent time to place the students in new random groups. Follow the procedure described in the IMP *Teaching Handbook*, and record the groups and the suit for each student.

2. Discussion of *Homework 9: Penny Weight*

"Do you think the weights of pennies are normally distributed?"

Ask students if they think that the weights of pennies are normally distributed. (This specific set of data is not, but it is likely that the variation among pennies, though slight, creates an approximately normal distribution.)

*"Do you think
Uncle Jack's coin
is counterfeit?"*

Then ask how many students thought the coin was counterfeit. Of those who did not think the coin was counterfeit, ask what weight would convince them that it was counterfeit.

Explain that although statistics will not tell them if the coin is counterfeit, it can tell them something about the probabilities involved. That is, it will tell them how rare such a weight is for a legitimate coin.

Bring out that there is considerable "fuzziness" in decisions like this; for example, there is no mathematical way to take Uncle Jack's personal reliability into account. But, even without this sort of factor, there is always a subjective component to interpreting statistics.

Tell students that they will soon be learning a statistical tool that will help them make these kinds of decisions.

> Students will learn about standard deviation in this unit. They will learn a different tool, called the *chi-square* *statistic,* in the Year 2 unit *Is There Really a Difference?*

3. *Mean School Data*
(see facing page)

Today's activity, *Mean School Data,* continues the process of helping students to decide what is unusual, and does so back in the context of the pendulum.

In this activity, students are given fictitious pendulum data from two high schools. The two sets of data have the same mean, but one set is more dispersed than the other. You can let students just dive right into this activity, and then discuss their conclusions.

4. Discussion of *Mean School Data*

*"What are the two
means? How well
do they represent
the data?"*

Ask volunteers to give you the two means. Then ask the class if they think that using the mean is a good way to represent each set of data. Students should see that there are some limitations to the use of the mean. Although the two sets of data have the same mean (1.22), they also have differences that the mean does not show.

Ask students to explain how the two sets of data differ. Try to elicit terminology such as "more dispersed" or "more spread out" to describe the King High data in comparison to the Kennedy High data.

*"Which periods do
you consider ordinary?
Which do you
consider rare?"*

Ask the club card members of a few groups to explain their group's decision on Question 2. You may want to ask them which periods they would

Mean School Data

Students at Kennedy and King High Schools were trying to determine what would affect the period of a pendulum.

At each school, students decided on standard pendulum characteristics for their initial experiments, including the length, weight, and amplitude.

Then five groups in each school took a fixed number of measurements of the period of this standard pendulum and calculated the mean for those measurements. The tables below give the mean pendulum periods found at each school.

Kennedy High

Group	Mean Pendulum Period (in seconds)
1	1.21
2	1.25
3	1.22
4	1.19
5	1.23

King High

Group	Mean Pendulum Period (in seconds)
1	1.16
2	1.22
3	1.31
4	1.11
5	1.30

Continued on next page

consider ordinary and which ones they would consider rare. The underlying question should be:

> *For each set of data, if changing the weight of the bob does not change the period of a pendulum, what are the chances of getting a period as far or farther from the mean as 1.29 seconds?*

Tell the class that mathematicians have a way to measure those chances, and they will learn about it tomorrow.

Classwork

The Pit and the Pendulum

1. Find the overall mean for each school's data.

2. One group from each school decided to test whether changing the weight of the bob would change the period of a pendulum, so they conducted the set of experiments again with a different weight. Both groups now got a mean pendulum period of 1.29 seconds.

   If you were at Kennedy High, what would you conclude? If you were at King High, what would you conclude? In each case, explain your reasoning.

Homework 10   An (AB)Normal Rug

One day, Al and Betty got bored playing spinner games and decided to try rug and dart games.

Betty thought that playing on square or rectangular rugs would not be challenging enough, so she made some rugs that looked like normal distributions. As usual, each point in the rug had an equally likely chance of receiving a dart.

As shown in the diagram at the right, each rug consisted of three parts, with a central portion placed symmetrically between the other two. The central part of each rug resembled the area under the normal curve between two vertical lines symmetric around the mean. This part of the rug used one design. The two outer portions of the rug used a second design, and resembled the area under the normal curve to the left or right of such vertical lines.

Al and Betty then tried to guess where the dart would land. One guessed it would land in the central portion of the rug (the part using the first design), and the other guessed it would land outside this central part (in a portion of the rug using the second design).

1. The diagrams below are like the rugs used by Al and Betty, with the shaded area representing one design and the unshaded area representing the second design. In each case, estimate what percentage of the area is shaded.

   a.

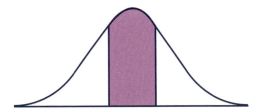

Continued on next page

Homework 10: An (AB)Normal Rug

b.

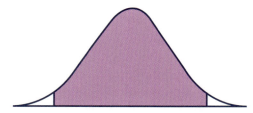

2. Trace each of the three rugs below. Then use two vertical lines to create regions like those above, to fit the condition in the next paragraph, and shade the region in the center. (Your shaded areas should each be centered around the vertical line of symmetry of the rug.)

Your task is to estimate where to put the vertical lines so that a player who guesses that the dart will land in the shaded area wins twice as often as a player who guesses it will land in the unshaded area. Also, explain how you determined that one area is approximately twice as large as the other.

a.

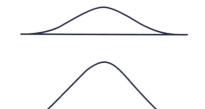

b.

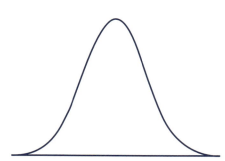

c.

3. Make another copy of the three rugs in Question 2, and repeat the process described there, except this time make the player with the shaded region win 95% of the time. Again, explain how you estimated the areas.

Data Spread

Students examine specific methods of measuring data spread.

Mathematical Topics

- Using area estimates to understand the normal distribution
- Comparing amount of dispersion in different sets of data

Outline of the Day

In Class

1. Discuss *Homework 10: An (AB)Normal Rug*

2. *Data Spread*
   - Students compare data sets with the same mean in terms of how "spread out" they are from the mean

- This activity will be discussed on Day 12 together with *Homework 11: Dinky and Minky Spread Data*

At Home

Homework 11: Dinky and Minky Spread Data

Special Materials Needed

- Overhead transparencies of the diagrams from *Homework 10: An (AB)Normal Rug* (see Appendix B)

Discuss With Your Colleagues

Don't Lose Your Place!

It's easy for students, and for teachers, to lose sight of the big picture in this unit. Discuss the overall plan of the unit with your colleagues, so that you understand where things are headed and how they fit together.

Also discuss ways to help students keep the big picture. Some of your experience from the unit *The Game of Pig* might be useful.

1. Discussion of *Homework 10: An (AB)Normal Rug*

You can use Question 1 to verify that students understand the idea of area under a curve.

Data Spread

• Rinky, Dinky, and Minky understood how to find the mean of any set of data.
• But they also knew that one set of data could have the same mean as another but
• look quite different.

Continued on next page

Then turn to Questions 2 and 3. Let students use a transparency of the curves from the homework to share their estimates of where to put the borderlines for each problem. Ask them to explain how they made their estimates.

2. Data Spread

This activity will be continued in tonight's *Homework 11: Dinky and Minky Spread Data*. Together, the two assignments provide students a chance to

On one occasion, they looked at these four sets of data, each of which has a mean of 20.

$$\text{Set } A \quad 19, 19, 20, 20, 21, 21$$

$$\text{Set } B \quad 10, 10, 20, 20, 30, 30$$

$$\text{Set } C \quad 12, 13, 13, 27, 27, 28$$

$$\text{Set } D \quad 9, 20, 20, 20, 20, 31$$

1. Based on your own intuition, arrange the four sets of data from the set that is "least spread out from the mean" to the set that is "most spread out from the mean." Explain your reasons for the order you choose. (You and your group members may want to discuss this together, but each of you should make your own decision.)

Rinky, Dinky, and Minky were looking for a way to assign a number to measure how spread out from the mean a set of data was. They wanted a method in which the bigger the number, the more spread out the data set would be from its mean.

2. Rinky liked the idea of using the **range** of the data to measure data spread. To find the range, you just subtract the smallest number in the list from the largest one. For example, you find the range for set D by taking the difference $31 - 9$, which is 22.

   a. Find the range for each of the other sets of data.

   b. Based on Rinky's method, arrange the four sets of data from the set that is "least spread out from the mean" to the set that is "most spread out from the mean."

   c. Does your result from Question 2b change your mind about your answer to Question 1? Explain.

Note: You will learn about Dinky's and Minky's ideas in *Homework 11: Dinky and Minky Spread Data.*

develop their own ideas about *spread* for a set of data. *Data Spread* will be discussed tomorrow, together with tonight's homework.

Homework 11   Dinky and Minky Spread Data

In *Data Spread,* you saw Rinky's idea for measuring data spread. His two friends had other suggestions.

For your convenience, here are the sets of data from that activity:

> Set *A*   19, 19, 20, 20, 21, 21
>
> Set *B*   10, 10, 20, 20, 30, 30
>
> Set *C*   12, 13, 13, 27, 27, 28
>
> Set *D*   9, 20, 20, 20, 20, 31

1. Dinky proposed finding the distance of each number in the list from the mean and then just adding those distances to get a measure for data spread.

Continued on next page

Homework 11: Dinky and Minky Spread Data

In this assignment, students learn two other methods for measuring data spread and are asked to come up with their own method.

For example, in set *C*, because the mean is 20, the number 12 is 8 away from the mean. Similarly, each number 13 is 7 from the mean, and so on. So Dinky would assign the number 8 + 7 + 7 + 7 + 7 + 8, which is 44, to set *C*.

   a. Find the number that Dinky would assign to each of the other sets of data.

   b. Based on Dinky's method, arrange the four sets of data from the set that is "least spread out from the mean" to the set that is "most spread out from the mean."

2. Minky's idea was to ignore the highest and lowest data items, removing just one item at each end even if there were ties. Then, he said, one should find the remaining data item that's farthest from the original mean and use that distance to measure data spread.

   For instance, with set *B*, Minky would drop the lowest number (one of the 10's) and the highest number (one of the 30's), leaving just 10, 20, 20, and 30.

   Because the mean of set *B* is 20, the maximum distance from any of these numbers to the mean is 10. So Minky would assign the number 10 to set *B*.

   a. Find the number that Minky would assign to each of the other sets of data.

   b. Based on Minky's method, arrange the four sets of data from the set that is "least spread out from the mean" to the set that is "most spread out from the mean."

3. Examine your answers to Questions 1b and 2b, as well as the answer to Question 2b of *Data Spread*. Whose measure of data spread—Rinky's, Dinky's, or Minky's—is closest to the answer you gave in Question 1 of *Data Spread*? Explain your decision.

4. Invent a way to measure data spread that is different from these three. Describe how it works, and explain whether or not you think it is better or not.

Calculating Standard Deviation

Students continue to compare methods of measuring data spread and are introduced to standard deviation.

Mathematical Topics

- Developing ways to measure dispersion of data
- Calculating standard deviation

Outline of the Day

In Class

1. Discuss *Data Spread* (from Day 11) and *Homework 11: Dinky and Minky Spread Data*
   - Have groups discuss which method of measuring data spread they like best and why
2. Discuss use of absolute value to measure difference from the mean

3. Define **standard deviation**
   - Introduce the procedure for calculating standard deviation
4. Tell students that key ideas about standard deviation are summarized in *Standard Deviation Basics*

At Home

Homework 12: The Best Spread

1. Discussion of *Data Spread* and *Homework 11: Dinky and Minky Spread Data*

Ask groups to compare their personal ordering schemes, as well as the numerical results from the three methods (and any other method that they created for measuring data spread). Each group should decide on the method it likes best, and then the diamond card member of the group should report to the whole class.

While students work, check to see whether they seemed to have any trouble finding the appropriate numbers for each data set for Rinky's, Dinky's, and Minky's methods. If so, you can take some time to go over the mechanics of each method.

"Which data set seems to be the most spread out from the mean?"

Then have the class discuss as a whole which set of data seems to be the most spread out. The decision does not have to be made based on a statistical test, and the class need not reach agreement on this. Have them focus their discussion on *why* they think a set is the most spread out.

For homework tonight, they will be asked to make up two sets of data so that Rinky's method shows one set to be more spread out but standard deviation shows the other set to be more spread out. Try to make sure they understand what this means.

Students will need to refer to last night's homework when they work on tonight's homework, so they should keep the last assignment another day rather than hand it in now.

2. Using Absolute Value

Discussion of spread from the mean provides a nice opportunity to talk about absolute value. Ask someone to go over what he or she did in applying Dinky's method to data set *C:* 12, 13, 13, 27, 27, 28.

Use values above and below the mean (which is 20) to illustrate that, in some cases, you subtract the mean from the data item, but, in other cases, you subtract the data item from the mean.

"How could you find the distance from the mean the same way in all cases?"

Ask if anyone can think of a way to do the same thing all the time and still get the right result.

If needed, suggest that they think about the idea of absolute value. Point out that $|x - 20|$ (or $|20 - x|$) always gives positive answers and measures how far a number x is from 20, no matter whether x is greater than 20 or less than 20.

Introduce the commonly used symbol $\bar{x}$ (read as "x bar") for the mean, and use notation such as x_i for a data item. Then ask how one could write Dinky's method using this notation and the summation symbol.

Students often enjoy seeing all this notation put together as

$$\sum_{i=1}^{n} |x_i - \bar{x}|$$

Later you can compare this notation with the symbolic formula for standard deviation.

3. Calculating Standard Deviation

Point out that, if Dinky's number is divided by *n*, you get the *average deviation* from the mean; that number tells you, *on the average,* how far the numbers in the list are from their mean.

Introduce the term **mean absolute deviation** for this average, and have students express it using summation notation as

$$\frac{\sum_{i=1}^{n} |x_i - \bar{x}|}{n}$$

Try to get students to articulate what this expression measures, because it is a simplified version of what standard deviation will tell them.

Then tell the class that although mean absolute deviation is a good tool for measuring data spread, statisticians actually use something slightly different, called the **standard deviation**.

Give students the definition through the use of an example. We will use the data set from *Standard Deviation Basics:* the five numbers 5, 8, 10, 14, and 18.

Have each student follow along as you explain how to calculate the standard deviation, using these steps.

1. Find the mean.

2. Find the difference between each data item and the mean.

3. Square each of the differences.

4. Find the average (mean) of these squared differences.

5. Take the square root of this average.

(The steps above and the table below are included in *Standard Deviation Basics.*)

Comment: Students may choose to ignore the sign of each difference in step 2, in effect using the absolute value of the difference rather than the difference itself. Since the differences are squared in step 3, their signs do not affect the final result. You may want to bring this out in order to emphasize the similarity between standard deviation and mean absolute deviation.

If you think students are comfortable with the summation notation used earlier to represent the formula for mean absolute deviation, you can show students that the definition of standard deviation involves just two changes to that expression:

- Replacing $|x_i - \bar{x}|$ by $(x_i - \bar{x})^2$

- Taking the square root of the final expression

Thus, the formula for standard deviation is

$$\sqrt{\frac{\displaystyle\sum_{i=1}^{n}(x_i - \bar{x})^2}{n}}$$

This formula is also included in *Standard Deviation Basics*.

The symbol usually used for standard deviation is the lower case form of the Greek letter *sigma*, written "σ." (You should mention this symbol, because students will be looking for it on their calculators.) You can remind the class that the upper-case Greek sigma (Σ) is the summation symbol.
Note: The issue of the distinction between σ and *s*—the *sample* standard deviation—is discussed on Day 15.

IMP Teacher Steve Hansen reacts to students' brainstorming of what variables might affect the swing of the pendulum.

Organizing the computation into a table like the one below can be very helpful. The computation of the mean is shown below the table to the left. On the right below the table, step 4 of the computation of the standard deviation is broken down into two substeps: (a) adding the squares of the differences and (b) dividing by the number of data items.

x	$x - \bar{x}$	$(x - \bar{x})^2$
5	–6	36
8	–3	9
10	–1	1
14	3	9
18	7	49

sum of the data items = 55   sum of the squared differences = 104

number of data items = 5   mean of the squared differences = 20.8

$\bar{x}$ (mean of the data items) = 11 σ (standard deviation) = $\sqrt{20.8} \approx 4.6$

Finding Standard Deviation

Tell your students that the following important facts hold true whenever a set of data is normally distributed:

• Approximately 68% of all results will be within one standard deviation of the mean.

• Approximately 95% of all results will be within two standard deviations of the mean.

Illustrate these facts using the areas shown in the diagram below, included for students in *Standard Deviation Basics*. (A copy of this diagram is included in Appendix B for use in making an overhead transparency.)

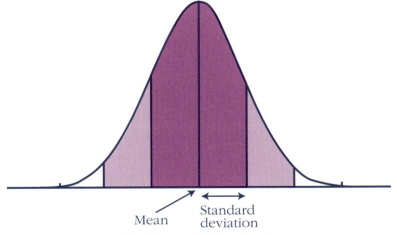

The Normal Distribution

In this diagram, the darkly shaded area stretches from one standard deviation below the mean to one standard deviation above the mean;

it is approximately 68% of the total area under the curve. The two lightly shaded areas represent data between one and two standard deviations from the mean.

The total shaded area stretches from two standard deviations below the mean to two standard deviations above the mean and comprises approximately 95% of the total area under the curve.

Note: In order to explain exactly where the specific numbers "68%" and "95%" come from, one would need a precise definition of normal distribution which involves calculus.

You should explain that the standard deviation provides a good rule of thumb for deciding if something is "rare."

- *Why not use mean absolute deviation?*

  Students may wonder why statisticians don't use mean absolute deviation— that is, just finding the average deviation from the mean. Here are two reasons for this decision.

  - Mean absolute deviation involves the use of absolute value, which is difficult to work with in calculus. Squaring differences from the mean and then taking a square root at the end turns out to be computationally easier than using absolute value.

  - Mean absolute deviation is more suitable if *median* is used instead of *mean* as the "central value." This distinction can be justified using basic algebra but will not be discussed here.

4. For Reference: *Standard Deviation Basics*
(see facing page)

These reference pages are provided to summarize for students the basic ideas about standard deviation.

You may want to have students read over this material as part of their homework. In particular, they should look at the material at the end, on the geometric significance of standard deviation, which has not been discussed today. (That portion is scheduled to be discussed with students tomorrow.)

Standard Deviation Basics

What Is Standard Deviation?

The **standard deviation** of a set of data measures how "spread out" the data set is. In other words, it tells you whether all the data items bunch around close to the mean or if they are "all over the place."

The superimposed graphs below show two normal distributions with the same mean, but the taller graph is less "spread out." Therefore, the data represented by the taller graph has a smaller standard deviation.

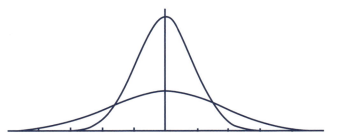

Calculation of Standard Deviation

Here is a list of the steps for calculating standard deviation.

1. Find the mean.

2. Find the difference between each data item and the mean.

3. Square each of the differences.

4. Find the average (mean) of these squared differences.

5. Take the square root of this average.

Organizing the computation of standard deviation into a table like the one on the next page can be very helpful. This table is based on a data set of five items: 5, 8, 10, 14, and 18. The mean for this data set is 11. The mean of a set of data is often represented by the symbol $\bar{x}$, which is read as "x bar."

Continued on next page

The computation of the mean is shown below the table to the left. On the right below the table, step 4 of the computation of the standard deviation is broken down into two substeps: (a) adding the squares of the differences and (b) dividing by the number of data items.

The symbol usually used for standard deviation is the lower case form of the Greek letter *sigma*, written σ.

x	$x - \bar{x}$	$(x - \bar{x})^2$
5	–6	36
8	–3	9
10	–1	1
14	3	9
18	7	49

sum of the data items = 55   sum of the squared differences = 104

number of data items = 5   mean of the squared differences = 20.8

$\bar{x}$ (mean of the data items) = 11 σ (standard deviation) = $\sqrt{20.8} \approx 4.6$

Suppose you represent the mean as $\bar{x}$, use n for the number of data items, and represent the data items as x_1, x_2, and so on. Then the standard deviation can be defined by the equation

$$\sigma = \sqrt{\frac{\sum_{i=1}^{n}(x_i - \bar{x})^2}{n}}$$

Standard Deviation and the Normal Distribution

The normal distribution was identified and studied initially by a French mathematician, Abraham de Moivre (1667–1754). De Moivre used the concept of normal distribution to make calculations for wealthy gamblers. That was how he supported himself while he worked as a mathematician.

But the normal distribution applies to many situations besides those that are of interest to gamblers. (Measurement variation is one important example.) Therefore mathematicians have studied this distribution extensively.

Continued on next page

When we use standard deviation to study the variation among measurements of a pendulum's period, we make this assumption:

> **Normality Assumption**
>
> If you make many measurements of the period of any given pendulum, the data will closely fit a normal distribution.

One of the reasons why standard deviation is so important for normal distributions is that there are some principles about standard deviation that hold true for any normal distribution. Specifically, whenever a set of data is normally distributed, these statements hold true.

- Approximately 68% of all results are within one standard deviation of the mean.

- Approximately 95% of all results are within two standard deviations of the mean.

These facts can be explained in terms of area, using the diagram "The Normal Distribution."

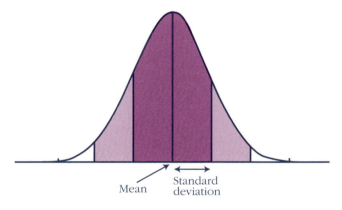

The Normal Distribution

In this diagram, the darkly shaded area stretches from one standard deviation below the mean to one standard deviation above the mean; it is approximately 68% of the total area under the curve.

The light and dark shaded areas together stretch from two standard deviations below the mean to two standard deviations above the mean, and constitute approximately 95% of the total area under the curve.

Continued on next page

So standard deviation provides a good rule of thumb for deciding whether something is "rare."

Note: In order to understand exactly where the specific numbers "68%" and "95%" come from, you would need to have a precise definition of *normal distribution,* a definition that is stated using concepts from calculus.

Geometric Interpretation of Standard Deviation

Geometrically, the standard deviation for a normal distribution turns out to be the horizontal distance from the mean to the place on the curve where the curve changes from being concave down to concave up.

In the diagram "Visualizing the Standard Deviation," the center section of the curve, near the mean, is concave down, and the two "tails" (that is, the portions farther from the mean) are concave up.

The two places where the curve changes its concavity, marked by the vertical lines, are exactly one standard deviation from the mean, measured horizontally.

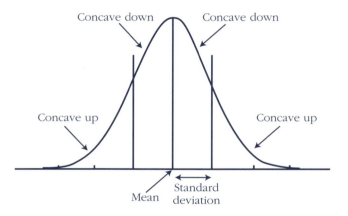

Visualizing the Standard Deviation

Homework 12   The Best Spread

Here are the four sets of data from *Data Spread*.

Set *A*   19, 19, 20, 20, 21, 21

Set *B*   10, 10, 20, 20, 30, 30

Set *C*   12, 13, 13, 27, 27, 28

Set *D*   9, 20, 20, 20, 20, 31

1. Write down the way you arranged the four sets of data in that assignment, from the set that is *least spread out from the mean* to the set that is *most spread out from the mean*.

2. a. Calculate the standard deviation of each set of data.

   b. Use your answers from Question 2a to arrange the four sets of data from the set with the smallest standard deviation to the set with the largest standard deviation.

3. a. Are the two arrangements, from Questions 1 and 2b, the same?

   b. If the arrangements are not the same, explain the reasoning you used in your arrangement from Question 1.

4. Recall that Rinky thought that *range* was a good method for measuring data spread. Make up two new sets of data, set *X* and set *Y*, in which set *X* has a larger standard deviation than set *Y* but set *Y* has a larger range than set *X*.

Homework 12: The Best Spread

This assignment will give you some sense of how comfortable students are with both standard deviation and the general idea of data spread.

Making Friends with Standard Deviation

Students explore how changes in data affect mean and standard deviation.

Mathematical Topics

- Comparing methods for measuring data spread
- Making geometrical interpretations of standard deviation
- Working with the idea of standard deviation

Outline of the Day

In Class

1. Select presenters for tomorrow's discussion of *POW 13: Corey Camel*

2. Discuss *Homework 12: The Best Spread*
   - Be sure students know how to compute standard deviation

3. Discuss the connection between standard deviation and the change in concavity of the normal curve

4. *Making Friends with Standard Deviation*
   - Students explore how changes in data affect the mean and the standard deviation

5. Discuss *Making Friends with Standard Deviation*
   - Let students share any conclusions they reached, but do not push for specific results

At Home

Homework 13: Deviations

Special Materials Needed

- Overhead transparencies of the diagrams in the section "Geometric Interpretation of Standard Deviation" (see Appendix B)

1. POW Presentation Preparation

Presentations of *POW 13: Corey Camel* are scheduled for tomorrow. Choose three students to make POW presentations, and give them overhead transparencies and pens to take home to use in their preparations.

2. Discussion of *Homework 12: The Best Spread*

As students come in, have them check their calculations on Question 2a within their groups. If there seem to be disagreements, you can have four volunteers each present the calculation of standard deviation for one set of data.

After the presentations on Question 2 by heart card members, you can decide whether discussion of Question 3 seems needed.

A discussion of Question 4 is optional. If students got stuck trying to come up with these data sets, you need not push on this issue. But, for students who are interested, you can suggest the supplemental problem *Data for Dinky and Minky,* which poses a similar question for Dinky's and Minky's methods of measuring data spread.

Make sure everyone in the class is clear on how to calculate standard deviation. If some students are having trouble, you can work with them while their groups begin the next activity.

3. Geometric Interpretation of Standard Deviation

As stated in *Standard Deviation Basics,* the standard deviation for a normal distribution is the distance along the horizontal axis between the mean and either horizontal coordinate for which the curve changes concavity. (The concept and language of concavity were discussed briefly on Day 7.)

"Based on this diagram, what is the relationship between standard deviation and the concavity of the normal curve?"

Ask students to look at the diagram "Visualizing the Standard Deviation" from *Standard Deviation Basics.* Have them describe in their own words the idea of concavity and its relationship to standard deviation.

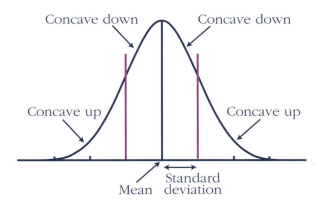

Visualizing the Standard Deviation

(Copies of this diagram and the next one are included in Appendix B for use in making overhead transparencies.)

As an illustration, have them estimate the standard deviation for the normal curve below, which has a horizontal scale marked on it.

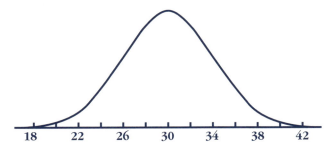

4. *Making Friends with Standard Deviation*

(see next page)

You can introduce *Making Friends with Standard Deviation* by telling students that before they explore how standard deviation relates to the unit problem, they need to gain more familiarity with the concept and with the mechanics of working with it.

As students work, you may need to push them to get started and to experiment with examples. For instance, some groups may need assurance that they can use any set of five numbers in Question 1a, and can use any nonzero number to add to the numbers in Question 1b.

Students' explanations in Question 1d may take several forms. They may picture the data points on the number line, so that adding the same thing to each point just moves the points along and hence also moves the mean. Or, they may see the change in the mean algebraically, although you should not expect a full algebraic explanation involving the distributive law.

Making Friends with Standard Deviation

You will be working with the concept of standard deviation in connection with the unit problem throughout the rest of the unit. Before you begin that work, it will be helpful for you to gain some more familiarity with the concept.

1. First, explore what happens to the mean and the standard deviation of a set of data when you add the same number to each member in the set.

   a. As a group, make up a set of five numbers that are all different. Find the mean and the standard deviation of your set.

   b. Now choose a nonzero number and add it to each member of your set. Find the mean and the standard deviation of your new set.

Continued on next page

Students may attribute the lack of change in standard deviation to the fact that the spread doesn't change when you move everything along. Or, they may see that the change in the mean cancels out the change in the data when you subtract.

The explanations for Question 2 should be similar. Question 3 is intended primarily as further work for groups that finish early.

    c. Repeat Question 1b, using a different nonzero number. Add this number to each member of your original set of data, and find the mean and standard deviation of the new set. Keep repeating this process until you see a pattern, and then describe that pattern.

    d. Explain why your pattern should occur.

- Explain why the mean changes as it does when you add the same thing to each member of the set.

- Explain why the standard deviation changes as it does when you add the same thing to each member of the set.

2. Now explore what happens to the mean and the standard deviation of a set of data when you multiply each member in the set by the same number.

    a. Begin with the same set of data as in Question 1a. Then choose a nonzero number other than 1. Multiply each member of your set by that number and find the mean and the standard deviation of the new set.

    b. Choose another nonzero number other than 1, and repeat what you did in part a.

    c. Keep choosing new nonzero numbers to use as multipliers for each member in your set. Find the mean and the standard deviation of each new set, until you see a pattern. Describe that pattern.

    d. Explain why your pattern occurs.

3. Make up a set of data for each of these pairs of conditions.

    a. Mean, 6; standard deviation, 1

    b. Mean, 10; standard deviation, 1

    c. Mean, 7; standard deviation, 2

5. Discussion of *Making Friends with Standard Deviation*

"What conclusions did you reach about how standard deviation is affected by changes in the data?"

In this unit, students will not have any need for the formal conclusions that arise from this investigation. It is more important that they have the experience of playing around and investigating the behavior of standard deviation.

Focus the discussion on parts c and d of Questions 1 and 2. Ask one or two spade card students to report on their groups' conclusions for these questions.

Margo Tuggle and Jennifer Balma discuss how changes in data affect standard deviation.

• •

Homework 13   Deviations

1. Find the mean and the standard deviation of this set of data.

24, 25, 15, 19, 17

Your task in the rest of this assignment is to make up new sets of data items, each having either the same mean or the same standard deviation as the data set in Question 1.

If you can, do these problems without actually calculating the mean or the standard deviation of each new set of data, and explain how you know without calculating that the data set fits the conditions.

2. Make up a set of five data items that has the *same mean* as the data set in Question 1 but has a *smaller standard deviation*.

3. Make up a set of five data items that has the *same mean* as the data set in Question 1 but has a *larger standard deviation*.

4. Make up a set of five data items that has the *same standard deviation* as the data set in Question 1 but has a *different mean*.

Homework 13: Deviations

This assignment provides students another opportunity to experiment with the idea of standard deviation and to develop their intuition about how it works.

POW 13 Presentations

Students present POW 13 and also continue work with data spread.

Mathematical Topics

- Continued work on standard deviation
- Using proportional reasoning to compare problems

Outline of the Day

In Class

1. Discuss *Homework 13: Deviations*
2. Presentations of *POW 13: Corey Camel*
   - Discuss the role of the mini-POW in helping students to solve the POW

At Home

Homework 14: Penny Weight Revisited

POW 14: Eight Bags of Gold
   - Students will share POW write-ups on Day 19, revise their write-ups for homework that night, and make presentations on Day 20

1. Discussion of *Homework 13: Deviations*

Have students share the data sets they made up within their groups. Then ask for volunteers to describe what methods they used to create the required data sets without calculating the means or standard deviations.

For your convenience: The mean of the data in Question 1 is exactly 20; the standard deviation is about 3.9. There are various ways to do Questions 2 through 4 without calculation. One approach on Questions 2 and 3 is to

> move the highest and highest and lowest values either both away from the mean or both toward the mean by the same amount. On Question 4, one method is to add some amount to all the data items.

"How does this homework relate to yesterday's class activity?"

You may want to ask students how this activity relates to yesterday's work on *Making Friends with Standard Deviation*.

2. Presentations of POW 13: Corey Camel

"Was anyone able to get more bananas to market?"

Have the three students make their presentations on the POW. Ask if any other students were able to get more bananas to market than any of the presenters; if so, discuss their solutions. If no one has come up with the maximum possible, let students know that there is a better answer (without telling them what that answer is or how to get it).

> *For your convenience:* Assuming fractional bananas and miles are allowed, the best Corey can do is to get $533\frac{1}{3}$ bananas to market. If fractions are not permitted, then Corey can still get 533 bananas to market.

"How might you know when you have taken the maximum possible number of bananas to market?"

Also ask if any students have thought about how they would know when they have determined the maximum possible number taken to market. If so, discuss their thinking. (If not, don't push it.)

"How did the mini-POW help with the POW?"

Finally, discuss the role that the mini-POW played in their work on the POW itself. Here are some questions you can use to focus the discussion.

• Was the mini-POW helpful? If so, how?

• Why was the mini-POW easier to solve than the POW itself (if it was)?

• What's special about the numbers in both versions of the camel problem?

• Could you make up another version (*SuperCamel?*) that you could solve automatically from what you already know?

Use students' comments to bring out that often a hard problem can be solved by first looking at a simpler version.

Homework 14   Penny Weight Revisited

In *Homework 9: Penny Weight*, you saw that Sarah and Tom had been weighing a bunch of pennies on a sensitive scale. For your convenience, here again are the results that they got (in milligrams).

2600	2604	2607	2610	2612	2615	2616
2617	2618	2619	2623	2623	2624	2625
2626	2627	2630	2631	2636	2637	

1. Compute the mean and standard deviation of these weights. Record all your computations clearly so you can compare results with others in your group.

   Remember the steps in finding the standard deviation.

   a. Find the mean.

   b. Find the difference between each data item and the mean.

   c. Square each of the differences.

   d. Find the average (mean) of these squared differences.

   e. Take the square root of this average.

2. Now reconsider the problem of the penny that Sarah's and Tom's Uncle Jack claimed was counterfeit. When Sarah and Tom weighed that penny, they got a weight of 2641 milligrams.

   a. Based on your results in Question 1, what can you say about the probability that a real penny would have a weight so far from the mean?

   b. Do you think that Uncle Jack's penny is real or counterfeit?

Homework 14: *Penny Weight Revisited*

Students are expected to do this assignment by making a complex set of individual calculations, rather than by using the automatic statistics tools of calculators. They will learn the calculator shortcut tomorrow. Tonight's work of grinding out the answer should help students appreciate the convenience of having the calculator do all the computations.

POW 14   *Eight Bags of Gold*

Once upon a time there was a very economical king who gathered up all the gold in his land and put it into eight bags. He made sure that each bag weighed exactly the same amount.

The king then chose the eight people in his country whom he trusted the most, and gave a bag of gold to each of them to keep safe for him. On special occasions he asked them to bring the bags back so he could look at them. (He liked looking at his gold, even though he didn't like spending it.)

One day the king heard from a foreign trader that someone from the king's country had given the trader some gold in exchange for some merchandise. The trader couldn't describe the person who had given her the gold, but she knew that it was someone from the king's country. Since the king owned all of the gold in his country, it was obvious that one of the eight people he trusted was cheating him.

The only scale in the country was a pan balance. This scale wouldn't tell how much something weighed, but it could compare two things and indicate which was heavier and which was lighter. The person whose bag was lighter than the others would clearly be the cheat. So the king asked the eight trusted people to bring their bags of gold to him.

Being very economical, the king wanted to use the pan balance as few times as possible. He thought he might have to use it three times in order to be sure which bag was lighter than the rest. His court mathematician thought that it could be done in fewer weighings. What do you think?

Continued on next page

Point out to students that they should keep track of all their computations for the homework so they can compare their results with others in their group and locate any computational errors fairly easily.

POW 14: *Eight Bags of Gold*

Make sure all of the students know what a pan balance is and how it is used to compare weights. Students are scheduled to share their POW write-ups

To answer this question, follow these steps.

1. Develop a scheme for comparing bags that will always find the light one.

2. Explain how you can be sure that your scheme will always work.

3. Explain how you know that there is no scheme with fewer weighings that will work.

Note: Each comparison counts as a new weighing, even if some of the bags are the same as on the previous comparison.

Write-up

1. *Problem statement*

2. *Process:* Describe how you found your answer and how you convinced yourself that your method works in all situations. If you think your answer is the best possible, describe how you came to that conclusion.

3. *Solution:* Describe your solution to the king's problem as clearly as possible. Then write a proof that your method will work in every situation. If you think that the king cannot find the lighter bag in fewer than three weighings, prove it.

4. *Extensions*

5. *Evaluation*

and write reviews of one another's work on Day 19. They will revise their POWs in *Homework 19: POW Revision*, and presentations are scheduled for Day 20.

Deviation on the Calculator

Students use graphing calculators to do statistical computations.

Mathematical Topics

- Sample standard deviation—the distinction between s and σ
- Entering data and finding mean and standard deviation on a calculator

Outline of the Day

In Class

1. Discuss *Homework 14: Penny Weight Revisited*
   - Have students articulate the assumption of normality in this problem
   - Use percentages of normal distribution as described in *Standard Deviation Basics*
2. Contrast sample standard deviation with σ
   - Explain the computational distinction, but don't expect conceptual mastery

3. Discuss standard deviation with calculators
   - Show students how to enter data and find statistical information on their graphing calculators
   - If time allows, have them figure out how to do statistical work on their scientific calculators

At Home

Homework 15: Can Your Calculator Pass This Soft Drink Test?

Special Materials Needed

- Overhead transparency of normal curve for penny weight distribution (see Appendix B)

1. Discussion of *Homework 14: Penny Weight Revisited*

Ask students to work in their groups to achieve a consensus on the answer to Question 1 and to begin sharing ideas on Question 2.

Once students have agreed on the value of the mean (which is 2620 mg) and on the standard deviation (approximately 9.9 mg), ask for volunteers to present their answers and explanations for Question 2.

This is the first application of the percentages on standard deviation given in *Standard Deviation Basics,* so students may be somewhat unclear about the reasoning. The goal here is for them to see that, because the weight of the uncle's penny is more than two standard deviations from the mean, the chance of getting a result this far (or farther) from the mean is less than 5%.

Ask the class what assumption they are making in using this percentage. They should see that they are assuming that the distribution of weights among pennies is approximately normal. You can assure them that this is a reasonable assumption. Tell them that the percentages in *Standard Deviation Basics* refer only to normal distributions.

• *Is this result reasonable?*

"Does 9.9 seem about right for the standard deviation?"

Also ask students whether the value of 9.9 mg for the standard deviation seems reasonable. As needed, use the question to review the idea that standard deviation measures, more or less, a kind of average distance from the mean (although it is not literally an average).

Students should agree that, because some of the pennies are less than 10 mg from the mean and others are more than 10 mg from the mean, a standard deviation of 9.9 seems about right. You might ask them to actually calculate the average distance from the mean—that is, the mean absolute deviation— which is a variation on "Dinky's method" from *Homework 11: Dinky and Minky Spread Data*.

• *Sketching a normal curve to fit the situation*

"Sketch a normal curve with mean of 2620 and standard deviation of 9.9."

Ask students to draw a sketch of a normal distribution with a mean of 2620 and a standard deviation of about 9.9 and to shade the 5% area that they are discussing.

The diagram should look something like this.

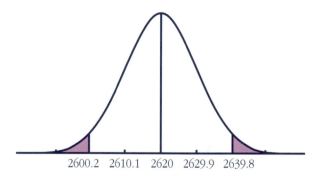

(An enlarged version of this diagram is included in Appendix B for use in making an overhead transparency.)

Have students point out the region on their sketch where 95% of all measurements of real pennies should fall.

Note: Making diagrams like this will help prepare students for work with the chi-square significance test in the Year 2 unit *Is There Really a Difference?*

- ## *Looking back at "Homework 9: Penny Weight"*

Ask students to discuss their answers to Question 2b and to compare their thinking now with their conclusions in Question 2 of *Homework 9: Penny Weight*. Specifically, ask how helpful standard deviation was in making their decision.

Students may say that the decision was just as easy to make without the use of standard deviation, but they may be more confident or more knowledgeable about their decision when they use standard deviation.

2. Sample Standard Deviation: *s* versus σ

At this point, tell students that there is a complication they need to be aware of in their use of standard deviation.

Point out that the computation they did on the homework (for the penny weight data) gave them the standard deviation *of their sample data*. However, in evaluating the authenticity of the supposedly counterfeit penny, what they really should consider is the standard deviation of the set of weights of *all* pennies in the world.

If students point out that it's impossible to do this, you can ask what they suggest instead. Try to draw out the idea of *estimating* the standard deviation from a sample.

Tell students that, technically, the best estimate of the standard deviation of a population, based on a sample, is given by a slightly different calculation than the one they used. Specifically, rather than divide the sum of the squares by n (the number of data items), one divides by $n - 1$, a smaller number. The statistic calculated in this way is usually represented by the letter s and is called the **sample standard deviation**.

Point out that, if n is reasonably big, s and σ will be only slightly different. Using s means dividing by a slightly smaller number, so that you get a slightly larger estimate for the standard deviation of the distribution. Tell students that they will see the difference in a moment, when they learn how to let their calculators do all the messy numerical work.

Note: Situations based on theoretical probability provide examples in which σ is more appropriate than s in working with standard deviation. Students will see such a situation in the Year 4 unit *The Pollster's Dilemma*.

3. Calculating Standard Deviation with Calculators

Demonstrate to the class how to use the statistics capability of their graphing calculators to find the mean, standard deviation, and sample standard deviation of the penny weights. Students may find the techniques somewhat difficult to learn, but they will probably agree that this alternative is preferable to doing the computation using just the arithmetic keys of a calculator (or—perish the thought—hand computation!).

Students should see in the course of this work that, for the penny weight data, $\sigma \approx 9.88$ and $s \approx 10.14$, so these two values are the same to the nearest integer.

If time allows, have students to try to figure out how to find mean, standard deviation, and sample standard deviation on their own scientific calculators (assuming that their calculators have statistical capability).

- *Optional: Standard deviation of stride data*

Also, if time permits, you might have students use their calculators to find the mean and standard deviation of their data on students' strides. They can then determine whether the percentages given in *Standard Deviation Basics* seem to hold true.

Homework 15: Can Your Calculator Pass This Soft Drink Test?

(see facing page)

This assignment will give students an opportunity to use the basic percentages about standard deviation.

Homework 15   Can Your Calculator Pass This Soft Drink Test?

1. A soft drink company sells its beverage in one-liter bottles. (*Reminder:* A liter is equal to 1000 milliliters. The abbreviation for millileter is mL.)

   The machine that fills the bottles is not perfect. The amount of soft drink it puts into the bottles fits a normal distribution, with a mean of 1000 mL (fortunately) and a standard deviation of 5 mL.

   Continued on next page

If the filling machine puts more than 1005 mL into a bottle, the bottle will very likely spill when opened, causing customers to complain. If the machine puts less than 995 mL into a bottle, the amount in the bottle will be visibly less than it should be, causing customers to feel cheated.

A quality-control worker checks the bottles after they are filled and before they are sealed to see if they fit within the bounds of these conditions. If a bottle is either too full or not full enough, the worker removes the bottle from the assembly line to be corrected.

Approximately what percentage of bottles get removed from the assembly line?

2. A manufacturer of graphing calculators keeps track of the length of time it takes before the product is returned for repair. She finds that the mean is 985 days and the standard deviation is 83 days.

   She wants to set a time period during which her company will warranty the calculators—that is, a period in which they will replace them at no cost to the customer if the products do not function properly. She does not want to have to replace more than 2.5% of those sold.

   Assume that the number of days before calculators need repair is normally distributed. How many days' warranty would you advise her to give her customers? Explain your reasoning.

3. Students' scores on a certain college entrance examination follow a normal distribution, with a mean of 490 and a standard deviation of 120. The college of your choice, Big State University, accepts only students whose scores on this test are 600 or higher.

   Estimate the percentage of students who are eligible for admission to Big State on the basis of their test scores, and explain your reasoning.

Days 16–20

This page in the student book introduces Days 16 through 20.

A Standard Pendulum

It's been a while since you actually measured the period of a pendulum, but now you have some statistical tools—normal distribution and standard deviation—to understand the variation in measurements that can occur even if you don't change the pendulum.

Over the next few days, you will get back to measurements, and use these tools to decide "what matters?" In other words, you will figure out, statistically, what variable or variables really affect the period of a pendulum.

Darrell Cabacungan and Aaron Gago try out the experiment from the supplemental problem "Are You Ambidextrous?"

The Standard Pendulum

Mathematical Topics

- Using standard deviation and the normal distribution in problem contexts
- Establishing a point of reference against which to measure change

Outline of the Day

In Class

1. Discuss *Homework 15: Can Your Calculator Pass This Soft Drink Test?*
   - Review the use of the percentages and discuss the idea of a "one-tail" situation
2. Review the status of the unit problem
   - Students should begin to see that they can use standard deviation to find the factors that determine the period of a pendulum

3. *The Standard Pendulum*
   - Students gather data about the period of a reference pendulum
   - Review how to measure the period
   - Compile and have students copy the list of results for use in tonight's homework
   - No other whole-class discussion of this activity is needed

At Home

Homework 16: Standard Pendulum Data and Decisions

Special Materials Needed

- Overhead transparency of normal curves for problems from *Homework 15: Can Your Calculator Pass This Soft Drink Test?* (see Appendix B)
- Experiment materials

1. Discussion of Homework 15: Can Your Calculator Pass This Soft Drink Test?

You can ask club card students from different groups to explain each problem.

On Question 1, students should refer to the fact (from *Standard Deviation Basics*) that in a normal distribution, approximately 68% of all results occur within one standard deviation of the mean. Therefore, about 68% of the bottles should pass inspection by the quality-control worker. In other words, 32% will need to be removed for correction.

"How is Question 2 different from Question 1?"

You may want to point out that Question 2 is set up in an opposite manner to Question 1. That is, Question 1 provides boundary or cutoff values and asks for a percentage, whereas Question 2 starts with the percentage and asks for a cutoff value. Specifically, the manufacturer wants to set a cutoff time so that only 2.5% of all calculators will need repair before that time. Students will probably use a diagram of the appropriate normal curve to illustrate what this cutoff time should be.

The problem in Question 2 is complicated by the fact that it involves only one "tail" of the normal distribution. The horizontal axis of the diagram below shows the mean as well as the values one and two standard deviations above and below the mean. The shaded portions of the area represent results that are at least two standard deviations from the mean. (Enlarged versions of this and the next diagram are included in Appendix B for use in making an overhead transparency.)

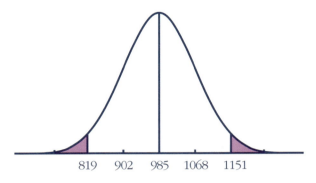

819   902   985   1068   1151

If students understand the percentages for standard deviation properly, they will see that the two shaded areas *together* total 5% of all calculators. Thus, the calculators that break down before 819 days constitute about 2.5% of the total. (Approximately 95% will break down somewhere between the 819th and the 1151st day; another 2.5% will last more than 1151 days.)

In other words, if the manufacturer offers to replace calculators that break in less than 819 days, then about 2.5% will need replacement.

Question 3 combines features of the first two problems. Like Question 1, it provides the cutoff value and asks for a percentage. Like Question 2, it is a "one-tail" problem; that is, it is concerned only with the percentage of students whose scores are above a certain value.

Question 3 is complicated by the fact that the difference between the cutoff and the mean is not a whole-number multiple of the standard deviation.

Again, a diagram is probably useful. In the diagram below, the shaded region is the area between the mean and one standard deviation above the mean. Students should be able to see that this area represents about 34% of all results.

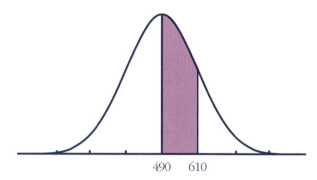

490   610

Thus, about 16% of students get scores above 610, and the percentage getting scores above 600 is slightly higher.

Don't get bogged down by the fine points of estimating the percentage of scores above 600. Although this is an interesting question, it is not the intended focus of this assignment. You can tell students that there are tables that provide details on areas like these so that people don't have to make visual estimates every time they come across a problem of this type.

2. Where Are We Now?

To get students to connect the concepts of normal distribution and standard deviation to the unit problem, you can ask them to do focused free-writing on the following topic:

Where are we now in the process of solving the unit problem?

Then ask them to share their ideas. They should see that they have completed the development to step 1 that was added on Day 9: "Give numerical meaning to *ordinary* and *rare*."

In other words, standard deviation is the desired numerical meaning, and the last two homework assignments (*Homework 15: Penny Weight Revisited* and *Homework 16: Can Your Calculator Pass This Soft Drink Test?*) should have helped students see how this tool is used.

- *So what's next?*

"How can you apply standard deviation in order to find out what determines the period of a pendulum?"

Ask students how they should proceed in order to apply this tool to pendulum measurements and to complete step 1—that is, to figure out which variables affect the period of a pendulum.

They should see that they need to establish a point of reference: They can't talk about the period *changing* without having something from which it changes. In other words, the task is to establish a mean and standard deviation for a fixed pendulum. Then they can look at what happens to the period when the pendulum is varied.

"How would you state in your own words what's going to happen next?"

Because this is such a central idea for the remainder of the unit, you may want to have several students try to state it in their own words.

3. **The Standard Pendulum**

(see facing page)

Have students read the activity *The Standard Pendulum*. The one-washer/ 2-foot/20° pendulum will be the reference pendulum—all pendulums will be compared to it.

If it seems appropriate, have the class as a whole discuss what the plan is. Students should understand that they will first do some experiments using this standard pendulum, compile their data, and calculate what the mean and the standard deviation are for these experiments. They will then be able to use those values to judge the significance of changes when they vary the pendulum.

Then give students the overview that, once they have established the mean and the standard deviation, they will conduct experiments in which they will vary, one at a time, the weight, the length, and the amplitude of the pendulum to see whether these changes affect the period enough to be more than incidental measurement variation. (These other experiments are part of the activity *Pendulum Variations*.)

- *Standardizing the measurement process*

"How are you going to measure the period of a pendulum?"

The class needs to agree on exactly how they will measure a single period of a pendulum. In previous experiments, some students may have timed several swings and then divided by the number of swings, whereas others may have measured several individual swings and then averaged the results (see discussion of *Homework 1: Building a Pendulum*).

If necessary, remind them of their experience with other experiments, such as in *Homework 4: What's Your Stride?*, where they may have seen that it was more accurate to measure many strides and then divide by the number of strides measured to get a representative stride.

The Standard Pendulum

The pendulum that is illustrated below will be called the *standard pendulum* for the rest of the unit.

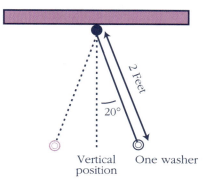

As you study whether changing a pendulum affects its period, you will be looking at pendulums that differ in some respect from this standard pendulum.

You will compare the periods of these other pendulums to the period of this one.

Here are the specifications for the standard pendulum.

- Weight of bob   1 washer
- Length of string   2 feet
- Amplitude   20°

Find the period of this standard pendulum using the procedure agreed upon by your class, and record your result.

Then repeat the experiment, again recording the period. Continue gathering more data as time allows.

The method to be used should be their decision, arrived at through discussion and perhaps based on their experiences with *Initial Experiments*. Record exactly what procedure they agree on, since they should use the same procedure throughout the rest of the unit.

You should also get students to clarify exactly how they will do other measurements. To determine the length of the pendulum, they should measure from the place where the string is attached at its top to the end of the washer. Also, emphasize that the amplitude is an angle measured *from the vertical*.

Technical note: You may wish to have students use a protractor to make a diagram like the one here (but much larger) on a sheet of paper, to be used for measuring the angles of their pendulums. Students may find it easier to use this sheet in setting up their pendulums than to use the protractors directly. (In *Pendulum Variations* on Day 17, students may want to use something similar with other angles marked on it, so have them save these sheets.)

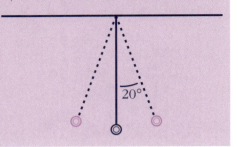

- *Doing the activity*

When the details of procedure and measurement technique have been worked out, have students work in their groups on the experiment described in the activity.

In order to get sufficient data to find reliable mean and standard deviation statistics, aim for a total of about 30 trials (although satisfactory results can probably be achieved with fewer trials).

You will need to give the students specific instructions about how many times to repeat the experiment.

As groups complete each experiment, have them write each period on a master list for the class.

In tonight's homework, students will work with this information, so they should copy the master list of estimates for the period before leaving class.

Homework 16: Standard Pendulum Data and Decisions
(see facing page)

This assignment will get students thinking about the issues that will be involved in *Pendulum Variations,* which they begin tomorrow.

Homework 16

Standard Pendulum Data and Decisions

You should have a large collection of measurements made for the period of the standard pendulum.

Although all groups worked with the same specifications for the pendulum, their results for the period probably were not all alike. In fact, each group probably came up with slightly different values each time they did the experiment to measure the period, even though the pendulum itself didn't change.

1. Why should different experiments using the exact same pendulum give different values for the period?

2. Make a frequency bar graph of the data you have, choosing intervals that you think are appropriate for grouping the data.

3. Draw a normal curve that approximates the graph you made in Question 2. Your curve should go approximately through the tops of the bars of your frequency bar graph.

4. Based on either your frequency bar graph from Question 2 or the curve from Question 3 (or both), estimate the mean and the standard deviation for the data.

5. Suppose you built a pendulum using different specifications, measured its period using the same procedure as in *The Standard Pendulum,* and got a result different from the mean you found in Question 4. How far from the mean would you need that new period to be before you were confident that the difference was not simply due to measurement variation? Explain your answer.

Pendulum Variations

Students examine how changes from the standard pendulum affect the period.

Mathematical Topics

- Summarizing experiment results and finding the mean and the standard deviation
- Developing a criterion for using standard deviation to make scientific decisions
- Conducting controlled experiments

Outline of the Day

In Class

1. Discuss *Homework 16: Standard Pendulum Data and Decisions*
   - Find the mean and the standard deviation of the data
   - Make a normal distribution graph based on this data, and save it for use on Day 18

2. *Pendulum Variations*
   - Students change one aspect of the standard pendulum at a time to determine if that variable affects the period

- Before the activity, decide as a class on a criterion for determining that a variable "matters" and post the criterion
- The activity will be discussed on Day 18

At Home

Homework 17: A Picture Is Worth a Thousand Words

Special Materials Needed

- Experiment materials
- Data from experiments in *The Standard Pendulum* on Day 16

1. Discussion of Homework 16: *Standard Pendulum Data and Decisions*

Let some students share their thoughts on Question 1. (This discussion should be a review of ideas about measurement variation that were developed earlier in the unit.)

Also, ask for comments about the frequency bar graphs that students created. If possible, get confirmation of the idea that the items of data are approximately normally distributed, and review the "normality assumption" stated on Day 7 and in *Standard Deviation Basics*.

Next, ask some volunteers to share their frequency bar graphs and accompanying normal curves, and to discuss how they used these items to estimate the mean and standard deviation. You might use this discussion as an opportunity to review the ideas in the section "Geometric Interpretation of Standard Deviation" (in *Standard Deviation Basics* and on Day 13).

• *Finding the mean and standard deviation*

Now have students enter the data in their graphing calculators and find both the mean and the sample standard deviation. Because the data here constitute a sample from "the world of measurements of the standard pendulum," it is more appropriate to use s, the sample standard deviation, than σ, the standard deviation of the actual data.

You may want to go over the distinction between σ and s to clarify that s is an estimate of the standard deviation for the distribution of all measurements of the period. Also, be sure students realize that the mean of their data from *The Standard Pendulum* is only an estimate of the actual period of this pendulum.

Once you have these estimates for the mean and standard deviation for measurements of the period of the standard pendulum, have the class sketch a normal distribution based on these values. You may want to put this sketch on a transparency for use in discussing *Pendulum Variations*.

• *Question 5 to be discussed after introduction of* Pendulum Variations

We suggest that you delay discussion of Question 5 from last night's homework until after students have looked at the next activity, *Pendulum Variations*.

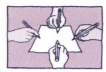

Pendulum Variations

You have seen that you may get slightly different results each time you measure the period of the standard pendulum.

As noted in *Standard Deviation Basics,* you are making this assumption about these measurement variations:

> Normality Assumption
>
> If you make many measurements of the period of any given pendulum, the data will closely fit a normal distribution.

In *Homework 16: Standard Pendulum Data and Decisions,* you estimated both the mean and the standard deviation of this normal distribution.

In this activity, you will look at what happens to the period if the pendulum is changed in certain ways. You will then use the results from this activity to decide what factor or factors seem to determine the period of the pendulum.

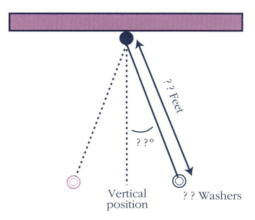

In conducting your experiments for this activity, you should measure the period in exactly the same way as you did in *The Standard Pendulum.* For example, if in that activity you measured the time for 10 swings and then divided by 10 to get the period, you should do the same thing here.

Continued on next page

2. *Pendulum Variations*

From today's activity, *Pendulum Variations,* students should realize that length is the primary factor in determining the period of a pendulum. This activity will be discussed tomorrow.

Make each measurement *twice,* but treat each as a separate result. *Do not average your two measurements!*

In each experiment, your pendulum should be the same as the standard pendulum except for the characteristic being studied in that case. Here again are the specifications of the standard pendulum.

- Weight of bob   1 washer

- Length of string   2 feet

- Amplitude   20°

1. *Changing the Weight*

Measure the period of a pendulum that is the same as the standard pendulum except that it has a weight of 5 washers.

2. *Changing the Length*

Measure the period of a pendulum that is the same as the standard pendulum except that it is 4 feet long.

3. *Changing the Amplitude*

Measure the period of a pendulum that is the same as the standard pendulum except that it has an amplitude of 30°.

- ## *Introducing the activity*

You can begin by referring to the list of variables that might affect the period of the pendulum (created on Day 2). Tell students that their work will focus on these three variables.

- Weight of the bob

- Length of the string

- Amplitude

You can list these variables under step 1 of the outline from Day 2.

Then have them read *Pendulum Variations*.

Note: The activity tells students to do each measurement twice, but not to average their measurements. The reason is that the standard deviation for a set of *averages* of data is different from the standard deviation for the data set itself. Because the sample standard deviation found earlier today was from individual experiments, students need to look here at results from individual experiments.

Students will learn about this issue in the Year 4 unit *The Pollster's Dilemma*.

• *Question 5 of the homework: Setting a criterion for concluding that a variable "matters"*

"How will you decide whether a given variable really affects the period of a pendulum?"

Finally, let students share their judgments regarding Question 5 from last night's *Homework 16: Pendulum Data and Decisions*. Emphasize that, although this is a subjective decision, they need to reach a class consensus, in advance of experimentation, on what criterion will be used to decide whether a given variable really affects the period of a pendulum.

For example, they may decide that, unless they get a result that is a particular number of standard deviations from the mean, they will assume that the given variable does not affect the period.

Caution students about the fact that each group is doing the experiment twice. If there are, say, eight groups, one would expect some of the 16 results to be more than one standard deviation from the mean *even if the groups used the standard pendulum*. So the criterion for deciding that something matters should certainly be stricter than having one group get a result that is more than one standard deviation from the mean.

In other words, students should decide on both *how far from the mean* a result must be to be significant, and *how many such results* they need within the class to conclude with confidence that the given variable matters.

Their criterion for deciding that a given variable "matters" could be some blend of these factors, such as getting either one result more than three standard deviations from the mean or two results more than two standard deviations from the mean.

Post the established criterion, and then have students begin their experiments.

Note: If you have students who think, for example, that going from one washer to five washers just isn't a big enough change, you can let them do other experiments of their own after they finish those described in the activity.

Homework 17

A Picture Is Worth a Thousand Words

It is said that "a picture is worth a thousand words." However, pictures, like words, can sometimes be misleading. This can be the case when people use graphs to make a point.

Graphs are pictures that convey information to people. And, just as there are people who forget to read the fine print in text, there are also people who don't look carefully at graphs to see what the numbers are really telling them. These people can be tricked into reaching false conclusions.

Here is an example. A television station wants to convince its advertisers that viewers are changing over to that channel in huge numbers. The station has experienced slow but fairly steady growth over the past year. If the station made a simple month-by-month graph of its ratings, this is what the graph might look like.

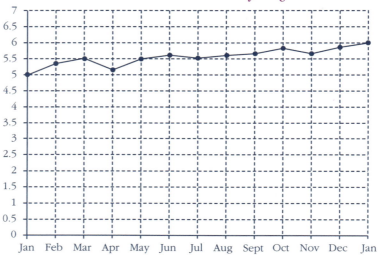

The Math Channel Makes Steady Progress!

As you can see, the station has increased its viewers by one ratings point, from 5.0 last January to 6.0 this January.

Continued on next page

This

Homework 17: A Picture Is Worth a Thousand Words

This assignment is somewhat tangential to the unit but is relevant in that it deals with how data can be used, or misused, to make a point.

It follows up on ideas begun in *Homework 12: The Issues Involved* from *The Overland Trail*.

• •

But there are many ways the graph can be changed to give the impression that the station is doing even better than it actually is.

One way is to show only part of the graph. The version below depicts only the changing part of the graph. It gives the appearance of a larger increase than does the graph above because the reader cannot see what the change relates to. The reader sees the graph starting at the bottom of the picture and ending at the top.

The Math Channel Adds Many Viewers!

The graph can be made even more dramatic by changing the scales of the axes so that the distance between 5.0 and 6.0 is greater. For instance, if you change the vertical scale so that each interval is worth 0.1 instead of 0.5, here is what the graph will look like.

The Math Channel Is Hot!

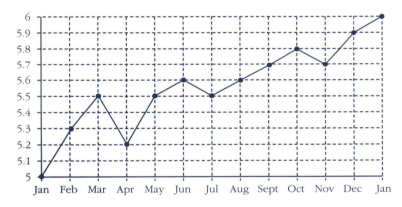

Continued on next page

Changing the horizontal axis can help too. In the next graph, the change is reported only every three months, so there are no "downs," only "ups." Making the graph line bolder also adds to the effect.

The Math Channel Is on Fire!

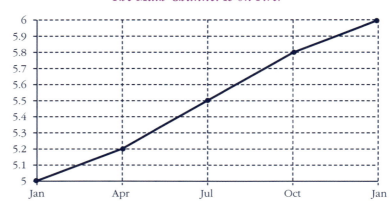

Your assignment

1. Create a misleading graph of your own. This actually requires that you make two graphs:

   a. an original graph

   b. a misleading graph

2. Describe the impact you were trying to create in Question 1. Explain how your graph is misleading.

3. Cut out a graph from a newspaper or magazine and write about why you think it is fair or why you think it may be misleading.

DAY 18

What Matters?

Students conclude that the period of a pendulum is determined primarily by its length.

Mathematical Topics

- Understanding how graphs can be misleading
- Continuing to work with standard deviation and controlled experiments

Special Materials Needed

- Normal distribution graph of standard pendulum data (from Day 17)
- Experiment materials
- 45° angles on sheets of paper (see Day 16)

Outline of the Day

In Class

1. Remind students that *POW 14: Eight Bags of Gold* is due tomorrow
2. Discuss *Homework 17: A Picture Is Worth a Thousand Words*
3. Discuss *Pendulum Variations* (from Day 17)
   - Consider each variable separately

- Have students share results and decide whether the variable affects the period

At Home

Homework 18: Pendulum Conclusions

1. *POW 14: Eight Bags of Gold* Due Tomorrow

Remind students that their POWs are due tomorrow. They will not make presentations, but instead will share their POWs with one another. You can tell them this, but emphasize that POWs must be completed tomorrow.

2. Discussion of Homework 17: *A Picture Is Worth a Thousand Words*

"What makes a graph more effective in producing a given impact?"

Ask students to share their graphs with their group members. They should discuss what factors make graphs more effective in producing a given impact. The diamond card student in each group should report to the class on the subjects of the graphs in her or his group, as well as on one or two factors the group considered effective in producing startling effects.

"Do you think it's ethical to use graphs like these?"

After discussing specific graphs in the assignment, you might ask students what they think about the ethics of using such graphs.

3. Discussion of *Pendulum Variations*

Have groups share their measurements of the different pendulums, focusing on one variable at a time.

Using a different color for each variable, mark each measurement on the graph (from Day 17) of the normal distribution of measurements of the period of the standard pendulum. (You may prefer to have three separate copies of this graph.)

As each variable is discussed, students should examine their collective results and compare them using the criterion established yesterday, prior to the activity. Although students may have already made up their minds based on their own group's experiments, you should insist that they use the common criterion.

• *Changing the weight*

"Does weight matter?"

Students should see that their results for the pendulum with a change in weight seem to fit well within the results that would be expected for the standard pendulum.

> If, for any reason, the class experiments seem to show that the weight of the bob does affect the period, you should probably tell students that physicists have shown that weight does not matter; thus, there is something going wrong in their experiments or mistaken in their analysis.
>
> For the rest of the unit, you can either rely on the truth of this physical fact or decide as a class what value to use for weight in order to control this parameter in later experiments.

• *Changing the length*

When class discussion turns to the change in length, students should see that this variable has dramatically affected the period of the pendulum. They should find that their results fulfill the criterion for "mattering."

Bring out that the decision that "length matters" is based on the fact that the results found would be extremely unlikely with the standard pendulum.

You can circle "length" on your list of possible factors and give a cheer.

• *Changing the amplitude*

The final experiment on amplitude poses the most difficult "Does it matter?" question.

An analysis based on the relevant laws of physics shows that changes in amplitude do affect the period of the pendulum, but the effect is very slight unless the angle exceeds 30° or so. For an increase from 20° to 30°, the change will probably be small enough to be within the measurement variation found for the standard pendulum. However, an increase from the standard 20° angle to a 60° angle might appear as a significant change in student experiments.

If the class experiments seem to show that amplitude does make a difference, then students will have to make some assumption about amplitude in order to solve the original question of the unit. In this case, tell the class to assume that the pendulum in the story had an amplitude of 20° and to use that value in their experiments on Day 25.

If the class does not find a difference in pendulum period based on change in amplitude, they will conclude that the period of a pendulum is determined by its length. You can tell them briefly that, in fact, very large changes in amplitude do affect the period, so that they do need to make some assumption as above.

• *Summary*

Have students make a chart summarizing their conclusions. If the experiments reflect the laws of physics, here is how the chart might look.

	Does It Matter?	How Much?
Weight	NO	—
Length	YES	A lot
Amplitude	YES or NO	Maybe a little, but not enough to be considered significant

It should be clear to the groups that the weight of the bob does not affect the period, the length of the string does affect the period, and the amplitude could (but probably doesn't) have a significant effect.

• *Revising the "Revised Question"*

Tell students that for the rest of the unit, they will assume that a pendulum's length determines its period. You may want to go back to the story to see that Poe's pendulum is "some thirty or forty feet overhead," and tell students that they will use 30 feet as the length of Poe's pendulum.

You can also go back to the original statement of the Revised Question (from Day 1) and revise it again, changing "Poe's pendulum" to "a 30-foot pendulum."

> The Revised Question
>
> *How long would it take for a 30-foot pendulum to make 12 swings?*

• *Now what?*

"What's next in solving the unit problem?"

Ask students where they are on the outline of steps for solving the unit problems. They should see that they have finally finished step 1 and are now ready for step 2.

Homework 18: Pendulum Conclusions
(see next page)

This assignment has two separate components. In Question 1, students write up and justify their conclusions from *Pendulum Variations,* using the concepts that have been developed in the unit. Tomorrow, they will share these write-ups, which will lead into their sharing of POW write-ups.

Question 2 asks students to grade their fellow group members based on their work during the experiments of the last few days.

Students may want to know if their group members will see the grades they assign. Some teachers think that students will be more honest in evaluating their peers if the evaluations are not shared with other group members. Other teachers think that it's important for this information to be shared.

You can either let the class decide this matter or you can decide for them. Tomorrow's discussion provides two options for handling this process, depending on the decision.

If students are not going to see one another's grades, then you should have them put the grades on a separate sheet of paper, since they will be sharing their work on Question 1 of this assignment tomorrow.

Homework 18   Pendulum Conclusions

1. In *Pendulum Variations,* you looked at what happened to the period of a pendulum when you changed from the standard pendulum. Based on those experiments, you have probably reached some conclusions about what factor or factors determine the period of a pendulum.

Summarize your conclusions clearly, and support them using the concepts of normal distribution and standard deviation.

2. In the experiments from both *The Standard Pendulum* and *Pendulum Variations,* you had to work closely with your fellow group members.

Decide what grade each member of your group deserves for the work he or she did in the last few days. Be sure to include yourself in this grading process.

In assigning a grade to each person, you may want to consider these factors.

- What suggestions the person made

- How well the person listened to others

- How supportive the person was to others

- Whether the person helped the group stay on task

- Whether the person helped the group when it got stuck

- Whether the person helped to settle disagreements in the group

- Whether the person ever helped the group reach a consensus

POW Sharing

Students share their write-ups of POW 14 and discuss what constitutes a good write-up.

Mathematical Topics

- Summarizing results on pendulum experiments
- Evaluating mathematical writing and reasoning

Outline of the Day

In Class

1. Discuss *Homework 18: Pendulum Conclusions*

   - Let students share their write-ups summarizing results from *Pendulum Variations*
   - Let students share ideas about group work

2. Students share write-ups for *POW 14: Eight Bags of Gold*

   - Students read and evaluate one another's write-ups

3. Select presenters for tomorrow's discussion of *POW 14: Eight Bags of Gold*

At Home

Homework 19: POW Revision

Discuss With Your Colleagues

Peer Grading

Reflect on how your students will feel about discussing the grades they assigned to themselves and to one another. Do you think it will be a positive experience for everyone? If not, is there something you could do to make it more positive? Decide how you will handle the homework discussion on Day 20.

In a similar context, discuss how to handle peer feedback on the POW write-ups on Day 20.

1. Discussion of *Homework 18: Pendulum Conclusions*

You may want to let students read one another's summaries of conclusions from *Pendulum Variations* and discuss their reasoning within their groups. (The sharing of homework here connects nicely with their sharing of POWs later today.)

This discussion should reinforce yesterday's conclusion that length is the major factor in determining the period of a pendulum.

Your handling of Question 2 depends on whether or not students will see one another's evaluations. Here are suggestions for both situations.

- If they do see the evaluations, this information can form the basis for a constructive discussion within groups about how to be a good group member.

- If they don't, the class can do focused free-writing on the topic "What my perfect group would be like." Afterward, you can ask volunteers to share what they have written.

In either case, after a while, you can lead a discussion on what students have learned about the components of successful group work. The discussion should lead the class toward the realization that cooperation and participation of all group members are essential for group success.

2. Sharing of *POW 14: Eight Bags of Gold*

There are at least two purposes to having students share their POWs with one another. First, they get to see other students' work—both good and poor. Second, they get feedback on their own POWs so that they can improve them.

There are many possible ways to shuffle POWs among the class. Here are a few.

- Collect them and then pass them back in a different order.

- Have group 1 pass to group 2, and so on.

- Make a chain by having each student pass the POW to the person on the right, except that one person from each group passes to the next group.

You can use any of these methods or one of your own.

- *What to do about students with no POW*

Your biggest problem will be what to do with those few students who did not bring their POW to class. A policy of "If no POW, then no POW reviewing" may probably be the fairest to those students who did bring their POWs.

Here are some options for students who did not bring their POW to class.

- They can read someone's POW after a reviewer has finished with it and is writing the review.

- They can write a one-page essay on why they didn't bring their assignment to class and why it couldn't possibly be avoided.

- They can just work on the POW.

If you use the first option, it may still be advisable for those who did not do a POW not to write a review; they will have significantly less time to do their critique and will probably be unable to do a good job.

- *Form of student reviews*

You can suggest that student reviews focus on "What I Liked About This POW Write-up" and "How This POW Write-up Can Be Improved."

Setting time limits for reading, reviewing, and exchanging papers will ensure efficient use of class time. Times will vary based on student reading and writing levels. Try to err on the "too much time" side so as not to frustrate those students who get involved in the process of reviewing.

3. POW Presentation Preparation

Give three students overhead transparencies and pens for preparing their presentations of the POW results. You may want to use your observations during the POW write-up sharing to choose students who are usually shy but who have done good jobs on the POW write-up.

Homework 19: POW Revision
(see next page)

Be sure that students understand their options to rework their POW write-ups.

Homework 19   POW Revision

Tonight you will revise your write-up of *POW 14: Eight Bags of Gold,* based on the feedback given to you by your classmates.

Your revision should be on paper *separate from your original,* and it can take many forms, depending on the feedback you received.

- You can redo your entire write-up.

- You can rewrite certain sections that need refinement.

- You can add additional comments and diagrams that would improve or clarify parts of your write-up.

After revising your write-up, write a paragraph on the value of reading other students' papers and getting feedback on your own paper.

In summary, you should bring four items to the next class:

- Your original write-up

- The reviews you received from your classmates

- Your revisions

- Your evaluation of the experience of reading other students' write-ups and receiving feedback on your own write-up

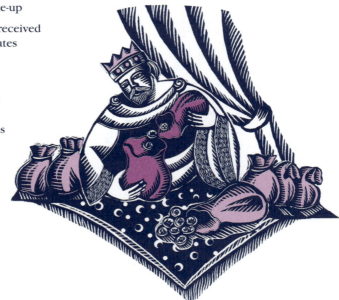

POW 14 Presentations

Mathematical Topics

• Logical thinking about situations with many possibilities

Outline of the Day

In Class

1. Form new random groups
2. Presentations of *POW 14: Eight Bags of Gold*
   • No discussion is needed of *Homework 19: POW Revision*
   • Challenge students to be sure that their solutions cover all cases

At Home

Homework 20: Mehrdad the Market Analyst

POW 15: Twelve Bags of Gold (due Day 28)

Discuss With Your Colleagues

What If No One Gets It?

POW 15: Twelve Bags of Gold **is a difficult POW. In many classes, few if any students arrive at an answer. Many teachers never arrive at an answer.**

Discuss some rationales for assigning such a difficult problem. Think about how you might feel if a student solves it but you do not. How would you handle the situation?

1. Forming New Groups

This is an excellent time to assign the students to new random groups. Follow the procedure described in the IMP *Teaching Handbook*, and record the groups and the suit for each student.

2. Presentations of *POW 14: Eight Bags of Gold*

Ask the three selected students to make their presentations on the POW. If any other students thought about the problem in a different way, have them explain their reasoning.

"Are you sure the scheme will always work?"

This is a good occasion to insist on completeness in the analysis, especially since students will have gotten a chance to share ideas to some extent in their POW reviews yesterday. This doesn't mean that the presenters themselves need to know all the answers; but the class should, collectively, be able to come up with a weighing scheme that will work no matter which bag is the light one, and they should be able to prove that it will always work.

Comment: It may not be clear to students what "always" means in this context. If they are confused, point out that the king doesn't know which bag is the light bag. Thus, when he does, say, his first weighing, the bags being weighed may include the light bag or may not; because he doesn't know, his scheme has to work in either case.

Challenge students with "What if…?" questions if they are leaving out possibilities and not challenging one another as needed.

"If you got stuck working on this problem, how did you get 'unstuck'?"

Since the next POW is similar to this one but much harder, it will benefit students to hear from others how they got "unstuck."

Here are some possible extensions that the class might discuss.

- What is the largest number of bags you could handle with only 2 weighings?

- What is the largest number of bags you could handle with only 1 weighing? 3 weighings? Is there a pattern?

If time remains after the POW discussion, have students begin work on *POW 15: Twelve Bags of Gold.* Be sure they grasp that, in this problem, they do not know whether the bag with counterfeit gold is lighter or heavier than the rest.

Homework 20

Mehrdad the Market Analyst

Mehrdad is a market analyst. He studies the relationship among an item's price, the number of items sold, and the amount of profit.

High price does not necessarily mean high profit. If a company sells a great product, but charges too much for it, the company will not sell very many units and therefore won't make very much profit.

On the other hand, low price does not necessarily mean high profit either. If the company sells the product for too low a price, it will sell a lot of units but will not be making much profit.

You can see the complexity. The ideal price is somewhere in the middle—not too low and not too high. Mehrdad studies the market and finds the most profitable price at which to sell an item.

Continued on next page

*Homework 20:
Mehrdad the
Market Analyst*

This homework is a lead-in to the curve fitting that the students will be doing to predict the period of a 30-foot pendulum.

• •

You have hired Mehrdad to analyze the market and suggest prices to charge in your music store. In particular, you have asked him to provide information about the price to charge for compact discs and compact disc players. Mehrdad comes back with this information.

Compact Discs

Price Charged (in dollars)	Expected Profit (in dollars per month)
11	–1100 (loss of $1100)
14	1800
17	1600
18	0

Portable Compact Disc Players

Price Charged (in dollars)	Expected Profit (in dollars per month)
100	0
115	1250
130	2000
150	–4000 (loss of $4000)

1. For each item, sketch a graph showing the relationship between different prices and the expected profit. (*Warning:* Be careful how you set up the scales on the axes.)

2. Sketch a line or curve that you believe represents the relationship between price and profit.

3. What price do you think will maximize the profit for each item? Explain your answers.

POW 15   Twelve Bags of Gold

Here we are back with our economical king. Thanks to your class's work on the *Eight Bags of Gold* POW, he found the thief in a very economical manner. Now, since he has been so economical, he has even more gold.

The eight bags got too heavy to carry, so he had to switch to 12 bags. Of course, each of his 12 bags holds exactly the same amount of gold as each of the others, and they all weigh the same. Well, . . . maybe not.

Rumor has it that one of his 12 trusted caretakers is not so trustworthy. Someone, it is rumored, is making counterfeit gold. So the king sent his assistants to find the counterfeiter. They did find her, but she wouldn't tell them who had the counterfeit gold she had made, no matter how persuasive they were.

Continued on next page

POW 15: Twelve Bags of Gold

Although this POW looks a lot like the last one, it is much more difficult. In fact, very few students have been able to solve it with three weighings, and many teachers have also been unable to do so.

So why is it included here?

All the assistants learned from her was that one of the 12 bags had counterfeit gold and that this bag's weight was different from the others. They could not find out from her whether the different bag was heavier or lighter.

So the king needed to know two things.

- Which bag weighed a different amount from the rest?

- Was that bag heavier or lighter?

And, of course, he wanted the answer found economically. He still had only the old balance scale. He wanted the solution in two weighings, as in the other problem, but his court mathematician said it would take three weighings. No one else could see how it could be done in so few weighings. Can you figure it out?

Find a way to determine which bag is counterfeit and whether it weighs more or less than the others. Try to do so using the balance scale as few times as possible. Keep in mind that what you do after the first weighing may depend on what happens in that weighing. For example, if the scale balances on the first weighing, you might choose bags for the second weighing different from the bags you would choose if the scale does not balance on the first weighing.

Note: The problem can be solved with only three weighings, without any tricks, but it is very hard to cover every case.

Write-up

1. *Problem statement*

2. *Process:* Based on your notes, describe what you did in attempting to solve this problem.

   - How did you get started?

   - What approaches did you try?

   - Where did you get stuck?

   - What drawings did you use?

3. *Solution:* Since this problem is much more difficult than *Eight Bags of Gold,* you shouldn't be too disappointed if you don't get a solution using just three weighings. Your task is to give the best solution that you found. Explain fully which cases your solution works for and which cases it doesn't work for.

4. *Evaluation*

Our experience is that many students, even if they do not find the optimal solution, still get pleasure out of the effort, and those who do solve it (perhaps a year or two after it is assigned) get enormous satisfaction.

The problem is sufficiently concrete that all students generally understand it and can work on it, despite its difficulty. They usually can find a solution using four weighings and can see many cases in which they can find the right bag (and identify it as heavy or light) in three weighings.

Take time to discuss the difficulty of the problem with students. You might mention your own experience with it, which may include not yet having the solution yourself and or having spent many months struggling to find it. You may want to tell them that the IMP teacher materials do not provide a solution.

It is important to strike a balance between, on the one hand, preparing students realistically for the challenge they face in this problem and, on the other hand, completely discouraging them from trying. You should also emphasize the importance of partial solutions. Let students know that there is as much mathematical learning to be gained in describing precisely the limitations of their solution as there would be in presenting a complete solution.

Even if you have a solution of your own, resist the temptation to provide hints on this problem. Its value lies not in the solution itself, but in the journey to find the solution.

This POW is scheduled to be presented on Day 28.

Days 21-24

Graphs and Equations

You're closing in on the unit problem. Now you know *what* determines the period of a pendulum, but you still need to figure out the relationship between the period and the controlling variable.

Pretty soon you'll gather some more data and look for a formula. In preparation for that, you're going to do a graphing "free-for-all"—an open-ended investigation of equations and their graphs—so you'll have an idea what kind of formula to try.

This page in the student book introduces Days 21 through 24.

The discoveries by Cody Boling, Ethan Fitzhenry, Lindsay Crawford, Catherine Bartz, Melyssa Brixner, and Nikki Robinson are fast and furious during "Graphing Free-for-All."

366

Interactive Mathematics Program

Ockham's Razor

Mathematical Topics

- Estimating a maximum value from a sketched graph
- Recognizing that many rules can be used to explain a given set of data
- Ockham's Razor

Outline of the Day

In Class

1. Discuss *Homework 20: Mehrdad the Market Analyst*

2. Review the status of the unit problem, bringing out the need to find an equation to fit a graph

3. *Bird Houses*
   - Students find a rule to fit a very simple situation

4. Preliminary discussion of *Bird Houses*
   - Go over the problem, and introduce a more complex version

5. Further discussion of *Bird Houses*
   - Bring out that there are various approaches and perhaps several solutions
   - Introduce Ockham's Razor as a principle for seeking the simplest explanation

At Home

Homework 21: So Little Data, So Many Rules

1. Discussion of *Homework 20: Mehrdad the Market Analyst*

Students should compare their homework answers and share how they decided on the best price to charge. Some students will probably connect the dots with line segments rather than with a smooth curve. If so, you can ask whether prices between those given in the tables would necessarily have profits on those line segments.

Students should see that they cannot tell for sure what price would give the maximum profit. If they just pick the price among those explicitly given that maximizes profit (that is, $14 for a CD, $130 for a CD player), you should ask whether a price slightly higher or lower might give a larger profit. (There is no definitive answer to this question.)

Don't ask students to formulate equations to describe the data here. That type of activity will be pursued later in the unit. You can tell them that one of the units next year (*Cookies*) will have a central problem about maximizing profits.

2. Using Graphs in the Unit Problem

Refer students to the outline from Day 2 and ask where they stand in the process. They should see that they are ready for step 2. Tell them that in a few days, they will collect data about pendulums of various lengths (in *The Period and the Length* on Day 25). They will be using this data set to try to predict the period of a 30-foot pendulum. Remind them of similar problems in *The Overland Trail,* in which they used data on consumption by groups of some sizes to predict consumption by groups of other sizes.

Also tell students that in preparation for the third part of the outline ("Looking for patterns and predicting"), they will be working for the next several days on more sophisticated ways of finding equations whose graphs go through specified data.

The purpose of this work is for students to be able to find a rule or an equation that describes how the period of a pendulum is related to its length. In order to learn how to find the right equation, they need to gain some experience and familiarity with how various kinds of equations work.

More specifically, they will be forming general ideas about a wide variety of equations, using their graphing calculators. This experience will be helpful in deciding how much and what kind of data to gather when they do their experiments on Day 25.

3. *Bird Houses*
(see facing page)

Present the class with the following seemingly elementary problem. Allow students to discuss the problem in their groups for just a few minutes.

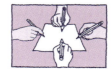

Bird Houses

Mia and her classmates in carpentry class had spent the semester constructing bird houses. Today Mia was in charge of painting. Her group had painted two of the bird houses after one hour of work, and six of them after three hours.

1. How many bird houses do you think they will have painted at the end of eight hours?

2. How can you generalize this answer?

4. Preliminary Discussion of *Bird Houses*

Have students share their conclusions with the class. No doubt they will have decided on an answer of 16 bird houses for the eight hours (for Question 1) and concluded, for Question 2, that the number of bird houses that can be painted is twice the number of hours (or something equivalent).

"What are some different ways to think about this problem and its solution?"

Ask them to organize and present their results and to discuss their thinking in as many ways as they can come up with. Their ideas should include

- An In-Out table

- A graph

- An equation

• *A complication about Mia*

Next present the following additional information that you just discovered:

> *At the end of five hours, Mia and her crew had actually painted only eight bird houses.*

"If they painted only eight bird houses in five hours, how many would they paint in eight hours? How can you generalize your answer?"

Ask students to discuss in their groups how this new information would change their answers to the original questions.

- How many bird houses will they have painted by the end of eight hours?

- How can you generalize this answer?

Emphasize that you want them to think in an open manner about *ways to approach the task,* rather than to get bogged down in details. Give them about ten minutes to work on this problem. Let them know that you don't necessarily expect them to find an equation that represents the problem.

5. Further Discussion of *Bird Houses*

Ask groups to report on what they did. Here are three approaches they may have tried.

- They may have applied previous ideas about approximating the data with a straight line. In other words, they may have looked for a linear graph or for an equation that would come close to fitting the information given.

- They may have tried to come up with a (nonlinear) function that would go through the three points $(1, 2)$, $(3, 6)$, and $(5, 8)$. However, it is highly unlikely that anyone found a function that fit the data perfectly.

- They may have plotted the points and then sketched a curve that passed through them.

As you discuss the groups' responses, emphasize two important points.

- There may be more than one good answer.

- Even if they didn't find an exact answer, looking for a different kind of rule is a good approach.

Point out that even when there were only two pieces of information (two bird houses after one hour; six after three hours), there were still other rules that might have worked. (For example, the equation $y = (x - 1)^2 + 2$ fits that information). The same is true for the three points. Just because a rule fits the data doesn't mean it must be *the* rule. People naturally think of the "two bird houses per hour" rule for various reasons, including these.

- It makes intuitive sense that Mia and her classmates should build the same number every hour.

- That is the simplest rule that fits the information.

- *Ockham's Razor*

    Tell the class about **Ockham's Razor.** This is a general principle in science that says

    > **Always explain things in the simplest possible way that fits the experimental information.**

    For example, it is said that the Polish astronomer Copernicus (1473–1543) decided to assume that the planets go around the sun (rather than that the sun and the other planets go around the earth) because he found that the equations describing the paths of motion were much simpler if he made that assumption.

    In the case of the original bird-house problem, the simplest explanation meant taking the "obvious" answer, "two bird houses per hour." In the context of the pendulum problem, it means that students will be looking for an equation whose graph comes reasonably close to their data points but is not terribly complicated. Discuss the fact that their pendulum data set is not absolutely perfect. Thus, it would be unreasonable to try to find an equation that fits perfectly.

Homework 21:
So Little Data,
So Many Rules
(see next page)

This assignment reinforces the ideas from the class discussion. If time permits, you can present an example for the whole class, using the pair *In* = 1, *Out* = 2. (Three possible rules are $y = x + 1$, $y = x^2 + 1$, and $y = 3x - 1$. Students can no doubt think of others.)

Students did problems like this in the *Patterns* unit, when they were first learning about In-Out tables. The work on *Bird Houses* gives such a problem the added significance of being connected to making a prediction.

Homework 21

So Little Data, So Many Rules

1. Consider an In-Out table with just one pair:

$$In = 2, Out = 5$$

   a. Find three rules that fit this pair.

   b. For each of the rules you find, find three pairs of numbers that fit that rule.

   c. Graph each of the rules that you made up.

2. Now repeat the steps in Question 1 for an In-Out table that has just this pair:

$$In = 4, Out = 2$$

Graphing Free-for-All

Mathematical Topics

- Function notation
- The relationship between equations and their graphs

Outline of the Day

In Class

1. Discuss *Homework 21: So Little Data, So Many Rules*
2. Introduce function notation
   - Summarize the four primary ways of thinking about functions
   - Express the unit problem in terms of function notation
3. *Graphing Free-for-All*
   - Students work in pairs to explore the graphs of various functions

- Begin to assign functions for poster presentations
- Students will complete the activity on Day 23 and make presentations on Day 24

At Home

Homework 22: Graphs in Search of Equations I

Discuss With Your Colleagues

Why a Graphing Free-for-All?

Discuss the purpose of the graphing free-for-all. What are the advantages of this approach? Wouldn't it be more efficient to give students a handout on different kinds of functions and their graphs? What would be accomplished by each approach in terms of student understanding and confidence?

1. Discussion of *Homework 21: So Little Data, So Many Rules*

"What are all the rules you found for each number pair?"

For each of the two questions, compile a list of all the different rules that students created to fit the given number pair. Using at least two or three examples for each question, have students give the other pairs they found that fit their rule and then plot these pairs.

If students seem interested, it would be helpful for them to see both linear and nonlinear examples for each case. In particular, try to draw out the rule $y = \sqrt{x}$ for Question 2, since a square-root function will be needed for their final pendulum analysis. But students will become aware of square-root functions in other ways before that, so you need not push this topic if it doesn't come easily.

2. Introduction of Function Notation

Take one of the examples from the homework discussion, and tell students that they are about to learn another way of expressing that function, called **function notation**.

Tell them that, with function notation, we give each function a name consisting of a single letter.

For instance, suppose that one of the rules used for Question 1 was the equation $y = 2x + 1$, and that a student found additional ordered pairs for this rule, creating this In-Out table.

In	Out
2	5
4	9
0	1
–2	–3

"Give me a letter of the alphabet."

Ask for a letter of the alphabet, and tell students that we could use that letter as the name of this function. (For this discussion, we will use the letter *b*.)

Thus, instead of writing $y = 2x + 1$, they could write the equation for the function as

$$b(x) = 2x + 1$$

Tell students that this equation can be thought of as defining "the *b* rule," and that the left side of the equation is read "*b* of *x*." (Some teachers prefer to read $b(x)$ as "the *b*-value of *x*." This is probably clearer, but it is not standard terminology.)

Mention that this notation is used for specific numerical values as well. For example, the fact that the numbers –2 and –3 are the *In* and *Out* for a row of the table for this function can be expressed by the equation $b(-2) = -3$. It *is* standard terminology to refer to –3 as "the value of the function b at $x = -2$" as well as simply calling it "b of –2."

"What is b(0)? b(7)?" Have students practice this notation and language by finding, for example, $b(0)$ or $b(7)$.

"What is b(t)? b(5w)?" Also include an example with another variable, such as $b(t)$, $b(*)$, or even $b(5w)$. Explain, as needed, that once the function b has been defined by the equation $b(x) = 2x + 1$, then it can be applied to anything. In other words, they can now find "b of anything" by multiplying the "anything" by 2 and then adding 1 to the result. For example, $b(5w)$ is, by definition, $2(5w) + 1$. (It is not important that students simplify this expression to $10w + 1$.)

Use similar examples to develop the insight that any letter can be used as the *In* to define the function. For instance, the equation $b(t) = 2t + 1$ defines the exact same function as the equation $b(x) = 2x + 1$.

Let students make up some letter combinations to stand for other functions from the homework. For example, they might write $h(x) = x + 3$ or $f(x) = 5$ for other solutions to Question 1, and $c(x) = x - 2$ or $g(x) = \sqrt{x}$ for functions that fit Question 2.

You don't need to spend a lot of time on this introduction of the notation; as it will be used more in this unit and will keep coming up in future units.

• *Four ways to think about functions*

"What ways do you know of to think about functions?" This new way to represent functions symbolically provides a good occasion to review the four approaches to functions that students have seen.

You can ask students what different ways they know of to think about functions. They should come up with all four.

- As a table of values (an In-Out table)

- As a graph

- In symbolic terms (as an equation or rule or, now, using function notation)

- In terms of a real-world situation

This complex of ideas should be familiar to students from *The Overland Trail* (see, for example, *Homework 13: Situations, Graphs, Tables, and Rules*), but it is worth summarizing again now, especially as a lead-in to connecting functions to the unit problem.

• *Function notation and the unit problem*

Ask students if they can think of a way to express the goal of the unit in terms of function language and notation. If necessary, ask them to express it in words first.

As discussed on Day 18, students have seen that the period of a pendulum is determined primarily by the length of the pendulum. So they may say that they want to figure out what they can do computationally when they know the length, in order to find the corresponding period.

"How can you express the goal of the unit in terms of function notation?"

You can ask students to suggest variables to represent a pendulum's length and period. Then have them express the goal of the unit in terms of function language and its notation.

For example, suppose they choose L and P to represent the length and the period, respectively. They might then express the goal of the unit like this.

> **Goal**   **To find an equation for a function f for which $P = f(L)$.**

Ask more specifically what they want to know about this function in terms of the exact situation in the story. As needed, remind them of their interest in the 30-foot pendulum. Since function notation is new to them, they may need help in formulating the goal in this notation. Help them as needed to see that their goal for the specific situation can be expressed like this.

> **Goal**   **To find $f(30)$, where f is the function that gives the period of a pendulum in terms of its length.**

They should see that if they have an equation or rule for $f(L)$, then finding $f(30)$ is just a matter of substituting 30 for L.

You can tell students that, broadly speaking, their method will be to make an In-Out table of combinations for L and P, based on experimental results, and then to find a rule or equation for that table. For now, they can just call that function f.

3. Graphing Free-for-All
(see facing page)

In this activity, students will experiment freely with graphs and the graphing calculators. The primary goal is for them to get a general sense of the shapes of the graphs of various families of functions. In particular, they will need to recognize that the set of data from Day 25's pendulum experiments (*The Period and the Length*) belongs to the square-root family of functions.

The activity is also intended to strengthen students' understanding of the connections among equations, tables, and graphs.

Even for functions that students haven't yet studied (such as the sine function), they can use the trace facility on their graphing calculators to find specific points. That is, even if they don't know what "sin x" means, they should understand that any point on the graph of the equation $y = \sin x$ has coordinates that belong in the table for the sine function.

Students will continue with this activity tomorrow and report on their results on Day 24.

Graphing Free-for-All

In this activity you will use a graphing calculator to explore the graphs of a variety of functions and equations. The understanding of graphs and their equations that you gain in this activity will help you to find the period of the 30-foot pendulum.

Take careful notes on the graphs you examine. You will be learning about other functions during presentations by classmates on this activity, and you will need to take notes on their presentations also.

You will summarize your own conclusions, as well as information from other students' presentations, in *Homework 24: Graphing Summary.*

For each of the equations you look at, your notes should include four kinds of information.

- The equation

- A sketch of the graph

- The viewing window you used on the graphing calculator

- A partial In-Out table, found both by using the trace feature on the graphing calculator and by substituting into the equation

You may find it helpful to put each example on a separate sheet of paper.

• What functions to study

Because students will need to know about the square-root function and its graph later in the unit, it is essential that at least some of them experiment with this function family as part of this activity. (Others will learn about it when students give reports on their results.)

On the other hand, you don't want to give away the fact that this is the crucial function for the pendulum.

One approach is to tell groups that, as part of their general exploration, they must include the graphs of each of these three functions and study variations on at least two of the three.

- $y = x$

- $y = x^2$

- $y = \sqrt{x}$

Take some time to discuss what is meant by "variations" here. Students may be able to guess, or you may need to give examples. For instance, you can tell them that variations on the function $y = x$ include functions such as $y = 5x$ and $y = x + 1$, and variations on $y = \sqrt{x}$ include functions such as $y = 2\sqrt{x}$, $y = \sqrt{5x}$, and $y = \sqrt{x + 3}$.

These specific families may take a lot of the class's time, but students should also look at some other functions of their own choosing.

You may want to remind students to experiment with zooming, so that they see more of the graph. This is important with, for example, trigonometric functions; students may not see much happening if they don't set an appropriate viewing rectangle. Since they probably don't know anything about these functions, they can find a good viewing rectangle only by experimentation.

- *Activity write-up, assignment of functions, and presentation preparation*

  Be sure to discuss with students the write-up and presentation aspects of the activity.

  Tell students that as they work, you will assign specific functions or families to different groups, and that they will need to prepare posters as assigned. (You should make assignments so as to illustrate different general shapes of graphs or categories of algebraic expressions.)

  Also tell them that they will report on these assigned functions on Day 24. However, they should be preparing these posters as they go, rather than waiting until they have completed their entire exploration.

  During the reports on Day 24, they will need to take careful notes on other students' results.

  In addition to these poster reports, students will write a final summary in *Homework 24: Graphing Summary*. You may want to mention that these write-ups will be included in students' portfolios for this unit.

- *Outline a sample poster*

  You might want to go through a simple example to show students what is expected on their posters. Use function notation as well as the "$y =$" notation.

Each poster should show an equation, its graph and the viewing rectangle used, and a partial In-Out table.

• *Students work in pairs*

We suggest that you have students work in pairs on this activity. Larger teams could be cumbersome for working on the graphing calculator.

Homework 22:
Graphs in Search
of Equations I
(see next page)

This is the first of a series of three homework assignments in which students look for the equations that fit given graphs. In this homework the graphs are all lines, but the other two will require quadratic equations.

Homework 22

Graphs in Search of Equations I

The coordinate system below shows three graphs, labeled *a*, *b*, and *c*.

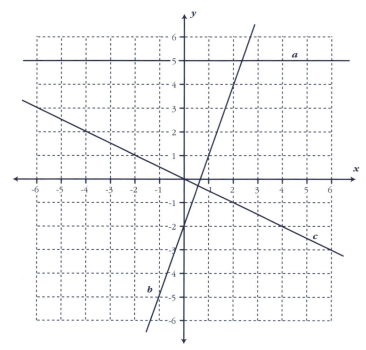

For each graph

- find four points that lie on that graph
- put the four points into an In-Out table
- write an equation for that table
- check that your equation seems to work for all of the points on the graph

Free-for-All Continuation

Students continue their exploration of equations and their graphs.

Mathematical Topics

- Continued investigation of graphs and their equations

Outline of the Day

In Class

1. Discuss *Homework 22: Graphs in Search of Equations I*
2. Students continue work on *Graphing Free-for-All* (from Day 22)
   - Finish assigning functions for poster presentations

At Home

Homework 23: Graphs in Search of Equations II

1. Discussion of *Homework 22: Graphs in Search of Equations I*

Students are working a lot with equations and their graphs in class, so you may choose simply to collect the homework at the start of class, without discussion. But graph *a* may need discussion, because its equation does not involve *x* at all. Having an In-Out table should be especially helpful here, since students will see that the *Out* values are all equal to 5.

2. Continued Work on *Graphing Free-for-All*

For the rest of today, students can continue working on *Graphing Free-for-All*. They should be preparing posters for tomorrow's presentations, and you will need to make assignments so that you get variety in the presentations.

Homework 23 Graphs in Search of Equations II

As with *Homework 22: Graphs in Search of Equations I,* the coordinate system below shows three graphs, labeled *a*, *b*, and *c*.

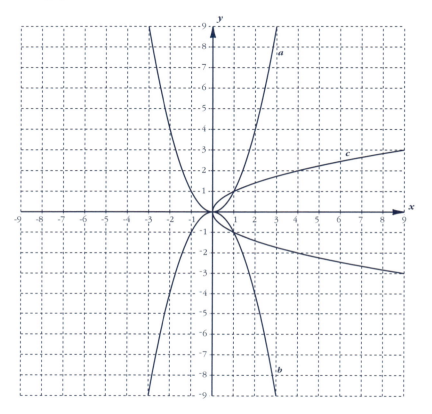

For each graph

- find four points that lie on that graph
- put the four points into an In-Out table
- write an equation for that table

Homework 23: Graphs in Search of Equations II

Tonight's *Graphs in Search of Equations II* has students look at graphs of basic quadratic equations.

Note: Graph *c* does not represent a function. You can bring this out in tomorrow's homework discussion.

Free-for-All Reports

Mathematical Topics

• Continued investigation of graphs and their equations

Outline of the Day

In Class

1. Discuss *Homework 23: Graphs in Search of Equations II*

2. Presentations of *Graphing Free-for-All* (from Days 22–23)

   • Have students organize the posters into families of functions with similar graphs

At Home

Homework 24: Graphing Summary

1. Discussion of Homework 23: Graphs in Search of Equations II

Ask students to share both their answers and their methods for obtaining those answers.

Students probably will not have trouble with graphs *a* and *b,* but they should be careful on graph *b* not to place the negative sign inside parentheses. That is, they should *not* write $y = (-x)^2$.

Note that graph *c* does not represent a function, because each positive *x*-value has two corresponding *y*-values. You may want to point this out. Students may represent this graph by the equation $x = y^2$, or they may see it as a combination of the graphs of the two equations $y = \sqrt{x}$ and $y = -\sqrt{x}$.

Discuss both approaches, eliciting the fact that the equation $x = y^2$ shows *x* as a function of *y* rather than the other way around. Tell students that we generally want functions to express the variable on the vertical axis in terms of the variable on the horizontal axis.

In particular, be sure students see that the upper half of graph *c*, by itself, is the graph of the equation $y = \sqrt{x}$. This example is especially important, because the data for the pendulum experiments (coming on Day 25) relating period to length should more or less fit an equation of the form $y = c\sqrt{x}$.

Students should realize that their calculators will draw graphs only for functions (although they can draw several graphs simultaneously on the same set of axes).

2. Presentations of *Graphing Free-for-All*

As pairs of students present their posters, create a display of various functions and their graphs around the classroom.

Each presenter should write down what the rest of the class should enter into their calculators in order to create the given graph. *Note:* Students may have different viewing rectangles on their graphs, in which case they will get different-looking graphs for the same equation.

It is important to take enough time after each presentation to allow listeners to add the sketch to the ones they found on their own. Each student can thereby create his or her own list of matching equations and graphs. You may want to remind the class that they will be summarizing all their findings in tonight's *Homework 24: Graphing Summary*.

Continue around the class until all pairs have presented their posters.

- *Putting it together*

At this point you will most likely have a chaotic collection of posters.

"How can you organize all of these graphs in a systematic way?"

Have the class rehang the posters into a systematic arrangement, grouping similar graphs together. Let students decide what "similar" means, as well as what other criteria to use for this organizing process.

They will be doing their own organizations and summaries for homework.

Homework 24: *Graphing Summary*
(see facing page)

This assignment provides students an opportunity to systematize what they have learned over the past three days about equations and their graphs. As noted earlier, students will include this assignment in their unit portfolios.

Homework 24 Graphing Summary

Through your work on *Graphing Free-for-All*, you should now have a collection of information about different equations and their graphs.

Your task now is to organize and summarize this information.

Create a summary document that will help you in the future to find an equation that fits a particular graph or to sketch the graph for a particular equation.

The Pit and the Pendulum

Days 25–28

Measuring and Predicting

**This page in the
student book
introduces Days 25
through 28**

Almost there! You're about to gather some data about the
periods for pendulums of different lengths. That sets the
stage for the final task—analyzing the data and making a
prediction for the 30-foot pendulum.

You might want to think about how you will test your
prediction.

*Principal
Robert
Embertson
makes a special
appearance as
the bob for the
final pendulum
experiment.*

Interactive Mathematics Program   373

Collecting Reliable Data

Mathematical Topics

* Continued investigation of graphs and their equations
* Gathering data in order to make a prediction

Outline of the Day

In Class

1. Discuss *Homework 24: Graphing Summary*
2. *The Period and the Length*
   * Students gather data about the periods of pendulums of different lengths
3. Discuss *The Period and the Length*

* Compile data into a single chart and post the chart for use on Day 26

At Home

Homework 25: Graphs in Search of Equations III

Special Materials Needed

* Experiment materials
* Optional: A ladder (for testing long pendulums in class)

1. Discussion of *Homework 24: Graphing Summary*

You probably don't need to discuss these summaries, unless students have questions or comments about their work.

The Period and the Length

Based on earlier work, you have determined that the period of a pendulum seems to be a function of its length.

Now you are going to gather some data about that function. Use the standard weight (one washer) and standard amplitude (20°), but vary the length.

For each length that you examine, find the time for *twelve* periods, since the prisoner in Poe's story thought there were about twelve swings remaining when he created his plan to escape.

374

2. *The Period and the Length*

Tell students that now that they have explored graphs, they are really ready to tackle step 2 of their Day 2 outline. That is, it's time for them to collect some data about the periods of pendulums of different lengths. (They will work on step 3 on Day 26.)

You might want to review the status of the problem. This review could depend on how your class dealt with the amplitude variable in the discussion of *Pendulum Variations* on Day 18. But however they resolved that issue, today's activity will treat only length as a variable, as indicated in that discussion.

Raise these issues with the class.

- How are they going to gather more data on length?

- How will they get reliable data?

- What factors are they going to hold constant so that only length varies?

As a class, decide on the different lengths that will be tested for period. Remind students that the more points they use and the wider the range of points, the harder it will be for several functions to explain their data.

Make sure students include both fairly long pendulums (such as 6 feet or 8 feet) and fairly short ones (such as 1 foot or 0.5 foot). Otherwise, their data may appear to lie in a straight line.

You probably shouldn't go beyond 10 feet or so, because the impact of being able to use the data to make a prediction will be more dramatic if the 30-foot pendulum is significantly beyond students' earlier results.

Assign several different pendulum lengths to each group, and have students perform the experiments. Students may have to tape pendulums from book cases or from the ceiling to have room for long pendulums.

Be sure students realize that the activity asks them to find the time for *twelve* periods, following the information in Poe's story.

3. Discussion of *The Period and the Length*

Be sure students collect all the data together in a single chart so that everyone can use it. You can post the data on a class chart, such as this.

Length of pendulum	Time for 12 periods

"What did you notice about the data?"

"Do you think the relationship is linear?"

Discuss the data, asking what students notice. Probably they will see that, as the length of the pendulum increases, so does the period. Ask if they think it is a linear relationship. Someone should suggest graphing it to find out.

Remind students that their goal is to figure out *from the data* how long it would take a 30-foot pendulum to make twelve swings.

You can also tell them that after they have completed their analysis, they will test it by building a 30-foot pendulum. You may want to spend some time

Homework 25 — Graphs in Search of Equations III

For each of the graphs *a* and *b* below

- find four points that lie on that graph
- put the four points into an In-Out table
- write an equation for that table
- check that your equation seems to work for all of the points on the graph

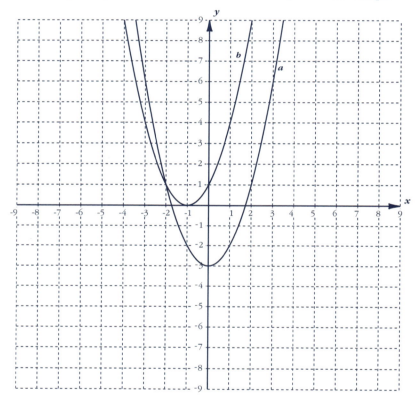

discussing how they will do this, because it will probably happen on the day after tomorrow!

Homework 25: Graphs in Search of Equations III

The graphs in tonight's homework are the most difficult in the *Graphs in Search of Equations* series.

Finding THE Function

Students look for a function to fit their pendulum data and predict the period of a 30-foot pendulum.

Mathematical Topics

- Curve fitting
- Using curve fitting to predict the results of an experiment

Outline of the Day

In Class

1. Discuss *Homework 25: Graphs in Search of Equations III*

2. *The Thirty-Foot Prediction*

    • Students use data from *The Period and the Length* to predict the period for a 30-foot pendulum

3. Discuss *The Thirty-Foot Prediction*

    • Have students share their predictions of the period, and post these predictions

At Home

Homework 26: Mathematics and Science

Discuss With Your Colleagues

How to Swing?

Discuss how you will handle Day 27 and the building of a 30-foot pendulum. If there is no convenient place for a 30-foot pendulum in your school, review the alternatives given in the Day 27 teacher notes.

You may want to arrange to do this activity once for all of your school's Year 1 classes.

1. Discussion of *Homework 25: Graphs in Search of Equations III*

Ask students to check their homework in their groups. If there is disagreement on answers, they should try to convince one another that they are right. They can use their graphing calculators to check the graphs.

If students are having difficulties and you want to pursue this topic further, you can ask what familiar graph these graphs resemble (namely, $y = x^2$) and how they differ from that graph and from one another. But this is not an appropriate place to get into a discussion of the general issue of transformation of quadratic functions.

During family IMP night, teacher Diana Herrington records the 30-foot predictions from students and their families.

The Thirty-Foot Prediction

Now that you have the data on the time required for 12 swings for pendulums of several different lengths, your task is to make a prediction for a 30-foot pendulum.

Look for a function *f* that fits all of your data as well as possible. You probably won't find a function that fits the data perfectly, but do the best you can.

Once you are satisfied with your choice of function, find *f*(30). That is, find out what your function would predict as the time required for 12 swings of a 30-foot pendulum.

2. *The Thirty-Foot Prediction*

Refer to the outline from Day 2. Students have finished step 1 (finding out which variable affects the period) and step 2 (collecting the data). They are now ready for step 3 (looking for patterns and predicting).

Remind students about the curve fitting they did using graphing calculators in *The Overland Trail*. Tell them that they are to use the same technique to analyze their pendulum data. You may want to review the general steps.

- Plot the data on the graphing calculator.

- Leave the data on the screen and graph a function that you think might approximate the data well.

- Examine how closely your function's graph approximates the data, and adjust the function until you think it approximates the data about as well as possible.

If students need a hint as they look for a function, you can ask if the graph resembles any of the examples from recent homework. Or, have them look at posters of work from *Graphing Free-for-All*.

3. Discussion of The Thirty-Foot Prediction

"What function did you find to fit the data?"

If students have accurate data with a wide enough range, with L representing the length of the pendulum and P representing the time for 12 periods, they should find that there is an equation of the form $P = c\sqrt{L}$, for some constant c, that closely fits their data. You may get several competing curves of this form, and the students need not agree on which is the best fit to the data.

"What is your prediction for the period of the 30-foot pendulum?"

Be sure also to collect the values that groups got for $f(30)$, and post them for comparison with tomorrow's experiment.

• *Is this a reliable method for prediction?*

You should raise the question of whether extending their data in this way makes sense. That is, do they have any reason to believe that the pattern of their data will continue as far as a 30-foot pendulum?

All you need to accomplish is to raise some skepticism. In this case, students' curve fitting should work well, but they should be aware that there is a complex issue here. The real test will come tomorrow.

Homework 26: Mathematics and Science
(see facing page)

Tell students that they will be asked to include tonight's assignment in their unit portfolios.

Homework 26

Mathematics and Science

Think about what you have learned in this unit, both in mathematics and in science. Choose what you consider to be the two or three most important ideas or concepts. Then, for each of those ideas or concepts

- write what you learned about that idea or concept
- write about a problem for which it might be useful to know that idea or concept

To Swing or Not to Swing

Students measure the period of a 30-foot pendulum and compare the results with their predictions.

Mathematical Topics

• Confirming the results of curve fitting

Outline of the Day

In Class

1. Select presenters for tomorrow's discussion of *POW 15: Twelve Bags of Gold*
2. Discuss *Homework 26: Mathematics and Science*

3. Build a 30-foot pendulum and find its period

At Home

Homework 27: Beginning Portfolios

Special Materials Needed

• Materials for building a 30-foot pendulum

Note: Discussion of *Homework 26: Mathematics and Science* can be postponed to Day 28 so that more time will be available for the construction of the pendulum.

1. POW Presentation Preparation

Presentations of *POW 15: Twelve Bags of Gold* are scheduled for tomorrow. Choose three students to make POW presentations, and give them overhead transparencies and pens to take home to use in their preparations.

2. Discussion of Homework 26: Mathematics and Science

Ask students to list things they have learned in the unit. Note each idea or concept on chart paper. Once all the topics have been listed and students have described what they learned about each, ask students to describe problems in which these ideas would be useful.

Have students retain to this homework for use in connection with tonight's assignment.

3. Building the 30-Foot Pendulum

You may want to review the predictions students made yesterday for the period of the 30-foot pendulum. Then have the class confirm or refute their predictions by actually building a 30-foot pendulum and timing its swings.

Take the class to a prearranged location and time 12 periods of a 30-foot pendulum. Go "Ooooh!" and "Ahhhh!" Then return to the classroom.

• *Options for creating a 30-foot pendulum*

If there is no location within your school building from which to swing a 30-foot pendulum, consider one of these options.

- Ask the fire department or a utility company if they can provide a truck from which the pendulum can be swung.
- Use the back of the bleachers in your stadium.
- Use the scaffolding in your gymnasium.

• *If you can't build a 30-foot pendulum*

If you can't find a way to set up a 30-foot pendulum, you should build a pendulum that is as long as possible. Before building it, have students predict its period using their functions from *The Thirty-Foot Prediction*.

Then build the pendulum and compare it with students' predictions. Even though it may be disappointing not to fulfill the conditions of the story, your pendulum can still serve to validate students' formulas and confirm the validity of the overall method.

• *Summary discussion*

"Did your predictions match the actual period?"

Discuss whether the functions students got on Day 26 accurately predicted the period of the actual 30-foot pendulum.

If they did not, discuss why not. Let students speculate as to why their method may have led them astray.

"Do you think the prisoner could have escaped in that amount of time?"

In a different vein, ask whether they think Poe's story is realistic. That is, would 12 swings of a 30-foot pendulum really provide enough time for the prisoner to escape?

You might ask students to close their eyes and try to estimate when a time interval has elapsed that is equal to the time they found for the 12 swings of a 30-foot pendulum. This exercise would give them a better idea of how long that time is.

• *Unresolved issues*

Ask groups to note some questions that arose in their study of this unit that were not resolved or some things they didn't really understand. You can have the heart card students report. List those items on chart paper.

Then discuss some of the issues that have arisen. Tell students that it is natural for some important ideas to seem fuzzy at first. As they study more mathematics and science, the ideas will become clearer. Bring out that many deep, powerful ideas are understood not through one experience but only after repeated exposure to them.

The amazement on students' faces as they saw their pendulum problem being verified by a fellow student hanging 30 feet in the air from a fire engine bucket was priceless.

IMP Teacher George Kirchner

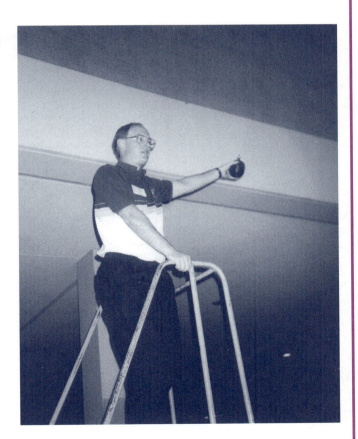

IMP teacher Dave Calhoun awaits the timekeeper's signal before letting go of the pendulum bob.

Homework 27   Beginning Portfolios

1. State the central problem for this unit in your own words. Then write a careful description of how you arrived at a solution for the problem. This description will serve as the cover letter for your portfolio for this unit.

2. In *Homework 26: Mathematics and Science,* you identified two or three key ideas or concepts from this unit.

   a. Describe the role that those ideas played in solving the unit problem.

   b. Select a class activity or homework that helped you to understand each of those ideas. Describe what you learned in those assignments.

Homework 27:
Beginning
Portfolios

Tonight students will complete the first stage of assembling their unit portfolios. Remind them to bring all of their work from the unit to class tomorrow so they can finish their portfolio work.

POW 15 Presentations and Portfolio Day

Students present POW 15 and also assemble their portfolios.

Mathematical Topics

* Logical thinking about situations with many possibilities
* Summary of the unit

Outline of the Day

In Class

1. Presentations of *POW 15: Twelve Bags of Gold*
2. *"The Pit and the Pendulum"* Portfolio
   * Students complete work on their portfolios for the unit

At Home

Students prepare for unit assessments

1. Presentations of POW 15: Twelve Bags of Gold

Ask the students selected yesterday to make their POW presentations. If other students had different ways of working with the problem, or arrived at a different solution, ask them to present.

If no one was able to solve the problem, suggest that they keep working on it. Certainly, you should acknowledge again to students the extreme difficulty of the problem.

"How are 'Twelve Bags of Gold' and 'Eight Bags of Gold' similar? How are they different?"

Ask if anyone can say how his or her work on *POW 14: Eight Bags of Gold* may have been helpful (or might be helpful in the future if they haven't yet solved the problem).

Discuss the similarities and differences between the two problems. Students will probably see that in the first problem they knew the bag they were looking for was lighter than the others, whereas this time they didn't know if it was heavier or lighter.

2. *"The Pit and the Pendulum" Portfolio*
(see facing page)

Tell students to read the instructions in *"The Pit and the Pendulum" Portfolio* carefully and then take out all of their work from the unit.

They will have written their cover letters and done part of the selection process in last night's homework. Today they need to finish choosing work and do the final portion of the portfolio.

You may want to mention to students that other units in later years of IMP will deal with the concepts of normal distribution and standard deviation. Thus, students should be sure to include material that is important to their understanding of these ideas.

If students do not complete the task in class, you may want them to take the materials home and finish compiling their portfolios for homework. Be sure they bring back the portfolio tomorrow with the cover letter as the first item. They should also bring any other work that they think will be of help on tomorrow's unit assessments. The remainder of their work can be kept at home.

Homework: Prepare for Assessments

Students' homework for tonight is to prepare for tomorrow's assessments by reviewing the ideas of the unit.

"The Pit and the Pendulum" Portfolio

Now that *The Pit and the Pendulum* is completed, it is time to put together your portfolio for the unit.

Cover Letter for "The Pit and the Pendulum"

Your work on Question 1 of *Homework 27: Beginning Portfolio Work* will serve as your cover letter for this unit.

Selecting Papers from "The Pit and the Pendulum"

Your portfolio for *The Pit and the Pendulum* should contain these items.

• Activities selected in *Homework 27: Beginning Portfolios*

Include your written work for Question 2 of this assignment as well as the activities from the unit that you selected.

• *Homework 26: Mathematics and Science*

• *Homework 24: Graphing Summary*

• A Problem of the Week

Select one of the four POWs you completed during this unit (*The Big Knight Switch, Corey Camel, Eight Bags of Gold,* and *Twelve Bags of Gold*).

• Other quality work

Select one or two other pieces of work that represent your best efforts. (These can be any work from the unit—Problem of the Week, homework, classwork, presentation, and so on.)

Continued on next page

Other Thoughts

In addition to the papers selected above, discuss these issues.

- How you liked doing science experiments in a mathematics class

- What ideas you learned about in the unit but would like to understand better

- How you felt about grading yourself and others on group work

- Any other thoughts you might like to share with a reader of your portfolio

Students do the in-class assessment and can begin the take-home assessment.

Special Materials Needed

• In-Class Assessment for "The Pit and the Pendulum"

• Take-Home Assessment for "The Pit and the Pendulum"

Outline of the Day

In Class

Introduce assessments

• Students do *In-Class Assessment for "The Pit and the Pendulum"*

• Students begin *Take-Home Assessment for "The Pit and the Pendulum"*

At Home

Students complete *Take-Home Assessment for "The Pit and the Pendulum"*

End-of-Unit Assessments

Note: The in-class portions of unit assessments are intentionally short so that time pressure will not be a factor in students' ability to do well. The IMP *Teaching Handbook* contains general information about the purpose of the end-of-unit assessments and how to use them.

Tell students that today they will get two tests—one that they will finish in class and one that they can start in class and finish at home. The take-home part should be handed in tomorrow.

Tell students that they are allowed to use graphing calculators, notes from previous work, and so on, when they do the assessments. (They will have to do without graphing calculators on the take-home portion unless they have their own.)

The assessments are provided separately in Appendix B for you to duplicate.

In-Class Assessment for "The Pit and the Pendulum"

Steve works in a hobby shop. He was looking at the relationship between the length of certain models and the amount of paint they require.

Here are some estimates he came up with:

Length of Model (in feet)	Amount of Paint (in ounces)
1	2
2	6
3	14
5	40

Assuming that this pattern continues, estimate how much paint would be needed for a model that is 10 feet long. Explain your reasoning.

Take-Home Assessment for *The Pit and the Pendulum*

A circus performer wants to ride a bicycle right up to a brick wall and stop dramatically very close to the wall without crashing.

She wants to know when to apply the brakes.

She doesn't want to try the experiment because she is afraid of crashing. She just wants to predict at what point she should hit the brakes. However, she also realizes that no matter how hard she tries to make the conditions the same every time, there may be some variation in the distance required to stop her bicycle.

Devise a plan to collect and analyze data that will allow her to make this prediction, and describe how she might use the data.

Use the ideas of the unit, discussing the variables to consider, the problems she will encounter, normal distribution, and standard deviation.

Homework: Complete *Take-Home Assessment for "The Pit and the Pendulum"*

Students should bring back the completed assessment tomorrow. As with all work at home, they may collaborate or get assistance, but they should report this fact as part of their write-up of the assessment.

Summing Up

Mathematical Topics

• Summarizing the unit

Outline of the Day

1. Discuss unit assessments
2. Sum up the unit

Note: The discussion ideas below are written as if they take place on the day following the assessments, but you may prefer to delay presenting this material until after you have looked over students' work on the assessments.

1. Discussion of Unit Assessments

Ask for volunteers to explain their work on each of the problems. Encourage questions and alternative explanations from other students.

• In-class assessment

Let volunteers present their ideas about different parts of this assessment. Students probably attacked the in-class assessment by making a graph by hand, finding a formula, and/or using curve fitting with a graphing calculator. Those methods are all good ones.

For your convenience: The equation $y = 1.6x^2$ gives a good approximation of the data in the problem.

• Take-home assessment

This is a good assignment to discuss and to give students an opportunity to do again. You may want first to collect students' work on the problem, mostly to see that they have attempted to deal with it.

Ask students to discuss what the circus performer wants to do and why. Make sure everyone understands the problem. Get students to suggest variables that will affect her performance. You do not need to write them down; it should be the students' responsibility to take down information they want to use.

Then ask students how normal distribution and standard deviation will come into play. If no one knows, you might ask students to do some focused free-writing on how standard deviation related to the pendulum problem. Then ask again.

Use questions to get students to see that measurement variation is an issue in both problems and that measurements of the same thing are normally distributed.

2. Unit Summary

Let students share their portfolio cover letters as a way to start a summary discussion of the unit. Perhaps having each group pass its letters to another group would be a good way to allow each student to read several letters.

Then let students brainstorm about what they have learned in this unit. This is a good opportunity to review terminology and to place this unit in a broader mathematics context. Here are some of the major ideas from the unit.

- Testing of the effects of variables by keeping everything else fixed

- Use of a frequency bar graph to examine data

- Normal distribution

- Standard deviation

- Use of calculators for curve fitting

After students have discussed what they learned in the unit, you might want to lead a discussion on what makes a good cover letter.

Supplemental Problems

This appendix contains a variety of additional activities that you can use to supplement the regular material of the unit. These activities are included at the end of the student materials and fall roughly into two categories.

- Reinforcements, which are intended to increase students' understanding of and comfort with concepts, techniques, and methods that are discussed in class and that are central to the unit

- Extensions, which allow students to explore ideas beyond the basic unit, and which sometimes deal with generalizations or abstractions of ideas that are part of the main unit

The supplemental activities are given here and in the student materials in the approximate sequence in which you might use them in the unit. The discussion below gives specific recommendations about how each activity might work within the unit.

For more general ideas about the use of supplemental activities in the IMP curriculum, see the IMP *Teaching Handbook*.

- ## *Poe and "The Pit and the Pendulum"* (extension)

    This research assignment can be given to students at any point in the unit. You may want to talk with students' English teachers about their work on this activity.

- ## *Getting in Synch* (extension)

    This activity presents the concept of *period* in a different context, through which students will explore some number theory. The problem can be assigned at any time, since the concept of period is introduced on Day 1. This concept will be treated further in the Year 4 unit *High Dive*.

    For whole-number periods, the problems in this activity are fairly straightforward, but for fractions, the issues get more interesting. (Question 3 hints at an idea that Greek mathematicians called **incommensurate numbers.** This refers to a pair of numbers that we would today describe as having a ratio that is an **irrational number.** Don't expect students to get the correct answer to this question.)

- ## *Octane Variation* (reinforcement)

    This problem gives students another context in which to look at the need for controlling variables. It can be used at any time after the discussion of *Homework 2: Close to the Law*.

- ## *Height and Weight* (reinforcement or extension)

    The emphasis in this activity is on the general process of investigation, not on the specific conclusions. Students should discuss the reasons why a simple functional relationship between weight and height is impossible.

    This assignment might be most appropriate after the discussion on Day 3 of *Initial Experiments*.

- ## *More Knights Switching* and *A Knight Goes Traveling* (extensions)

    These activities offer good follow-up investigations after the discussion of *POW 12: The Big Knight Switch* on Day 6.

- ## *Data for Dinky and Minky* (reinforcement)

    This activity is a follow-up to Question 4 of *Homework 12: The Best Spread*.

- ## *Making Better Friends* (extension)

    This activity extends students' work from Day 13 on *Making Friends with Standard Deviation*.

- ## *Mean Standard Dice* (reinforcement or extension)

    This activity gives students some practice with standard deviation. It also shows that doing the same experiment more times doesn't change either the mean or the standard deviation. Students may be surprised about the result for standard deviation in Question 3. This activity can be assigned at any point after the concept of standard deviation is introduced.

- ## *Are You Ambidextrous?* (extension or reinforcement)

    This is an experiment-based activity using the idea of standard deviation and involving reasoning similar to that needed in the main unit problem. You may want to use this activity either as preparation for *Pendulum Variations* or as a follow-up to that activity.

- ## *Family of Curves* (reinforcement or extension)

    This activity can be used with groups to extend or reinforce the *Graphing Free-for-All* on Day 22.

    Give each group the equation of a basic curve, such as $y = x^2$. Ask students to look at some simple changes that could be made in the equation, such as $y = x^2 + 2$ or $y = 3x^2$. Such similar equations are said to be in the same **family of curves**. Groups should explore how graphs vary among different members of the family and should make a poster showing their results. They can use graphing calculators or computers to assist with their work.

- *Green Globs and Graphing Equations* (extension or reinforcement)

   In the educational software called *Green Globs and Graphing Equations*, by Dugdale, S. and Kibbey, D., (1986), the user is shown a coordinate system with several "dots" plotted. (Each dot is a small circle around a point.) The user's task is to find an equation whose graph passes through as many of the dots as possible. The software includes an option to focus on quadratic equations, and this option is accompanied by a tutorial program.

   This software is available from Sunburst Communications in Pleasantville, NY for Apple II computers or IBM PCs. It provides an excellent extension or reinforcement of the curve fitting in this unit, and can be introduced around the time of the Day 22 activity, *Graphing Free-for-All*.

   Have students do the tutorial on quadratic equations and then play the game. If they get stuck, encourage them to make an In-Out chart and guess a rule. You may decide that your students do not need to complete the tutorial before playing the game.

   Note: There is no material in the student book for use of this software.

- *More Height and Weight* (extension)

   This problem follows up on the supplemental activity *Height and Weight* by giving the question a more specific focus. It also ties in with the problem of curve fitting. It can be used after Day 26.

Appendix

Supplemental Problems

This page in the student book introduces the supplemental problems.

Many of the activities in *The Pit and the Pendulum* involve experiments and data-gathering. In analyzing data from these experiments, you use the concepts of normal distribution and standard deviation. Another important theme of the unit is the study of functions and their graphs. Experiments, data analysis, and functions are some of the themes in the supplemental problems as well. These are some examples.

- In *Height and Weight* you are asked to plan and carry out an exploration of the relationship between two variables.

- *Making Better Friends* and *Mean Standard Dice* strengthen your understanding of mean and standard deviation.

- In *Family of Curves,* you look at how changes in a function lead to changes in its graph.

Poe and "The Pit and the Pendulum"

Learn more about Edgar Allan Poe, the author of the short story "The Pit and the Pendulum."

What was his life like? What else did he write?

Also, read the entire story, to discover how the prisoner came to find himself strapped to the table, and what happened to him after he freed himself from the danger of the descending pendulum. (You may recall that the excerpt closes with the words "For that moment, at least, *I was free*.")

Report on what you learned about Poe and the story.

Getting in Synch

Al and Betty are taking a break from their probability games, and have gone to the circus to ride on the Ferris wheels.

There are actually several different Ferris wheels at the circus. Al chose one of them, and Betty chose another.

Al and Betty each get on at the bottom of the Ferris wheels' cycles, and the two Ferris

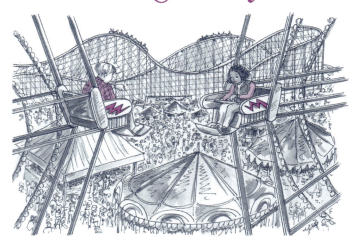

wheels start at the same time. The period of Al's Ferris wheel is 40 seconds; that is, it takes 40 seconds for it to make a complete turn. Betty's Ferris wheel has a period of 30 seconds.

1. How long will it be until the next time they are at the bottom together again?

2. Now redo Question 1 using each of the following combinations of periods for the two Ferris wheels.

   a. Al's, 40 seconds; Betty's, 25 seconds

   b. Al's, 31 seconds; Betty's, 25 seconds

   c. Al's, 23 seconds; Betty's, 18.4 seconds

3. Is it possible to find periods for the two Ferris wheels for which Al and Betty will never be at the bottom at the same time again?

4. What generalizations can you come up with?

Octane Variation

Elizabeth and her dad decided to find out if the number of miles per gallon their car got was affected by the type of gasoline they used. They decided to try three different grades of gasoline and measure the car's mileage for each.

When they began the experiment, the tank was filled with 87-octane gasoline. Elizabeth's dad drove until the tank was nearly empty. When he filled up the tank, he wrote down the octane of the gasoline he'd just been using, the number of gallons he'd used since the last fill-up, and the number of miles he had driven since the last fill-up.

He then went through the same procedure for each of the other two types of gasoline. Here is the information he presented to Elizabeth.

Octane used	Number of gallons used	Number of miles traveled
87	9.5	304
89	8.6	292
92	9.2	322

1. Given this information, do you think that the higher-octane gasoline yields better mileage? Explain your reasoning.

2. Elizabeth's brother Zeke thought there might be some other explanations for the variation in miles per gallon besides the octane of the gasoline. List all the other possibilities you can think of.

3. In what ways could Elizabeth and her dad have carried out a better experiment?

384

Height and Weight

In class, you are seeing that the period of a pendulum may be affected when different variables, such as length and weight, are changed.

In this activity, you will deal with variables in a different context. Specifically, you are to choose some setting in which to examine the relationship between *weight* and *height*. You are to design and carry out a plan for exploring how weight might depend on height in that context.

1. State the context of your exploration. (For instance, you may want to study how the weight of an animal depends on its height.)

2. Describe a plan for this exploration. For example:

   a. How will you gather information?

   b. What other variables will you take into account?

   c. What methods will you use to analyze your data?

3. Carry out your plan. That is, gather and study your data and come to some conclusions.

4. Describe your conclusions, evaluate the strengths and weaknesses of your plan, and discuss the difficulties involved in developing a connection between height and weight.

More Knights Switching

If you liked *POW 12: The Big Knight Switch,* here is a similar problem that is a bit more challenging.

This time there are three white and three black knights instead of two and two, and they are sitting on a board with four rows and three columns, as in the diagrams at the right.

The knights start in the positions shown in the top diagram. The goal is for the three black knights to change places with the three white knights, so that they end up as shown in the bottom diagram.

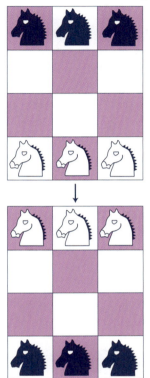

The knights are allowed to make only the same types of moves that they could make in the POW.

The big questions again are these.

1. Can they do it?

2. If so, what is the least number of moves it will take them to switch, and how do you know your answer is the least?

3. If it is not possible, explain why you are sure it is not.

Adapted from *aha! Insight,* by Martin Gardner, Scientific American, Inc./ W. H. Freeman and Company, San Francisco, © 1978.

A Knight Goes Traveling

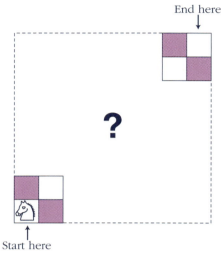

End here ↓

Start here ↑

If you like playing around with knight moves, here's one more problem for you.

In *POW 12: The Big Knight Switch*, you worked with four knights on a 3-by-3 chessboard, and in *More Knights Switching,* you worked with six knights on a 4-by-3 chessboard.

Now look at a single knight, and imagine placing that knight in one corner of a square chessboard of some unknown size, as shown at the left.

Here is the question for this problem.

> *How many moves will it take for the knight to get to the diagonally opposite corner?*

Of course, the answer depends on the size of the chessboard, and it may even be impossible for some cases.

Begin with a 2-by-2 board, then look at a 3-by-3 board, and gradually work your way up. Keep track of what the fewest possible moves is in each case, and look for patterns.

Data for Dinky and Minky

In *Homework 12: The Best Spread*, you were asked to make up two data sets, set X and set Y, that together fit these two conditions.

- Set X was to have a larger standard deviation than set Y.

- Set Y was to have a larger range than set X.

In other words, based on standard deviation, set X was to be more spread out, but based on Rinky's method, set Y was to be more spread out.

In this activity, you are to find two other pairs of data sets. In each case, deciding which set is more spread out will depend on the method used for measuring data spread.

1. Make up a pair of data sets, R and S, so that both of these statements are true.

   - Based on standard deviation, set R is more spread out than set S.

   - Based on Dinky's method, set S is more spread out than set R.

   Reminder: Dinky measures the spread of a set of data by finding the distance from each number to the mean and then adding those distances.

2. Make up another pair of data sets, U and V, so that both of these statements are true.

   - Based on standard deviation, set U is more spread out than set V.

   - Based on Minky's method, set V is more spread out than set U.

   Reminder: Minky measures the spread of a set of data by ignoring the highest and lowest data items, and then finding the largest distance from any remaining data item to the mean.

Interactive Mathematics Program

Making Better Friends

In *Making Friends with Standard Deviation*, you explored what happened to the mean and the standard deviation of a set of data when you added the same number to each member of the set or multiplied each member of the set by the same number.

In this activity you are asked to explore some other questions about mean and standard deviation. Here are some ideas to start you off.

1. How can you add new data items to a set so that you don't change the mean or the standard deviation?

2. How can you add new data items to a set so that you can keep the mean the same but make the standard deviation as large as you like?

Don't restrict yourself to these two questions. Make up some questions of your own and explore them. Report on everything you have discovered.

Mean Standard Dice

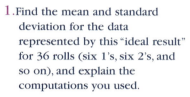

You know that, in the long run, a normal die will come up 1 one-sixth of the time, 2 one-sixth of the time, and so on.

Thus, for example, with 36 rolls, we'd expect about six 1's, six 2's, and so on.

1. Find the mean and standard deviation for the data represented by this "ideal result" for 36 rolls (six 1's, six 2's, and so on), and explain the computations you used.

2. Suppose the die were rolled 360 times, with the "ideal result" of 60 1's, 60 2's, and so on.

   a. Write down a guess about what the mean and the standard deviation would be for this set of data, and explain your guess.

   b. Actually find the mean and the standard deviation for this situation, and explain the computations you used.

   c. Are the actual mean and the actual standard deviation the same as in Question 1? Explain why you think they came out the same or different.

3. Now suppose you used a pair of fair dice, rolling them together and each time finding the sum of the numbers on the two dice.

   a. What would be the "ideal result" for these sums if the pair of dice were rolled 36 times? (That is, how many 12's would you get, how many 11's, and so on, as the sum of the pair of dice?)

   b. Write down a guess about what the mean and the standard deviation would be for this "ideal result" of 36 sums for a pair of dice, and explain your guess.

   c. Find the actual mean for this "ideal result." How does it compare to your mean in Question 1?

   d. Find the actual standard deviation for this "ideal result." How does it compare to your standard deviation in Question 1?

Are You Ambidextrous?

In this activity, you will compare the reflexes of your two hands. Here's how.

Have a partner hold a ruler vertically between your thumb and forefinger, so that the lower end of the ruler is level with your fingers. Spread your thumb and forefinger as wide apart as possible. Your partner should hold the ruler from its upper end.

Your partner will say "Drop" at the moment he or she drops the ruler. As the ruler falls past your fingers, you try to pinch it as quickly as you can.

1. Do the experiment with one of your hands 20 times, each time recording the place where you grab it.

2. Find the mean and the standard deviation of your data.

3. Draw a normal curve, with a horizontal scale, that has the same mean and standard deviation as your data. Show where the standard deviation marks are located.

4. Now do the ruler experiment one time with your other hand.

5. How many standard deviations from the mean was the experiment result from your "other" hand? What percent of the time do you think you would get a result that far from the mean using your "first" hand? Explain.

6. Do you think you are ambidextrous? Why or why not? (If you don't know what the word *ambidextrous* means, ask someone or look it up in a dictior

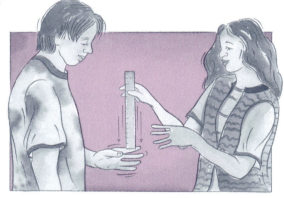

Family of Curves

You've seen that functions based on similar algebraic expressions often have similar graphs. For example, certain equations have graphs that are straight lines.

In this activity, your goal is to explore such **families of curves**.

Start with a simple function, such as $y = x^2$, and examine carefully how its graph changes as you make various changes in the equation itself.

Make a poster showing your results.

More Height and Weight

In the supplemental activity *Height and Weight*, you did a preliminary investigation of the relationship between the height and weight of objects.

In this problem, you will follow up with a more detailed investigation that looks specifically at the relationship between height and weight for people.

1. Find out the heights and weights for various people. Try to use individuals with a wide range of different heights, from small children to adults.

2. Make an In-Out table of your data, using height as the *In* and weight as the *Out*. Then make a graph of your data.

3. Try to find a formula that comes close to fitting your data.

4. Use what you've learned to estimate how much a 10-foot-tall person might weigh. Explain your reasoning.

For many of the discussions in this unit, you will find it helpful to have overhead transparencies of various diagrams. This appendix contains copies of these diagrams for your use in making such transparencies.

- For Day 7, four diagrams related to the normal distribution

- For Day 11, five diagrams from *Homework 10: An (AB)Normal Rug*

- For Day 12, the diagram from the section "Calculating Standard Deviation"

- For Day 13, two diagrams from the section "Geometric Interpretation of Standard Deviation"

- For Day 15, the diagram of the normal curve for penny weight distribution

- For Day 16, two diagrams for discussion of *Homework 15: Can Your Calculator Pass This Soft Drink Test?*

This appendix also contains copies of the in-class and take-home assessments for the unit.

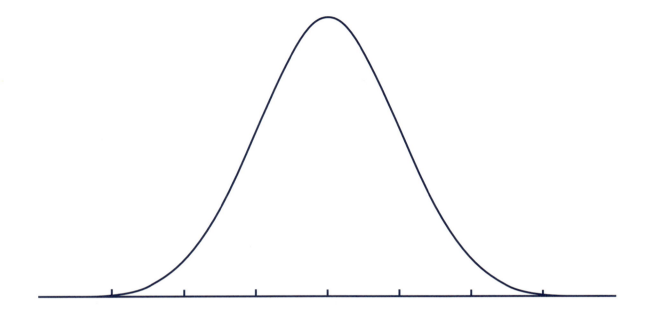

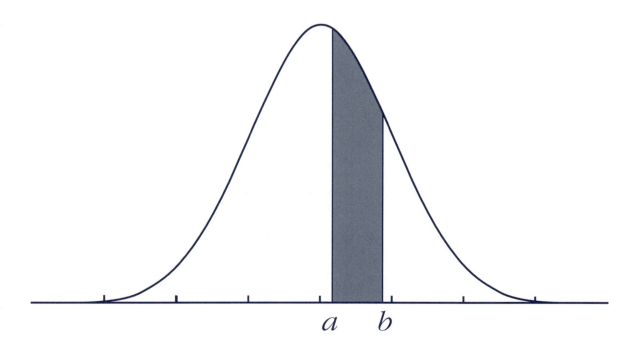

a b

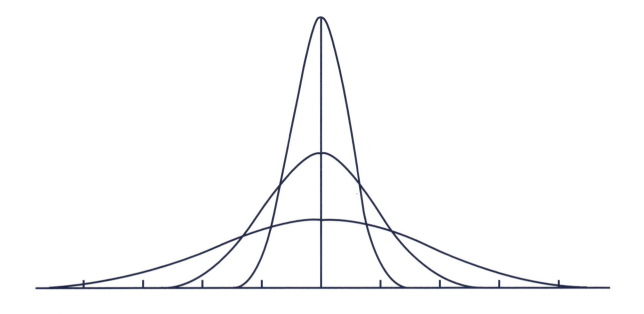

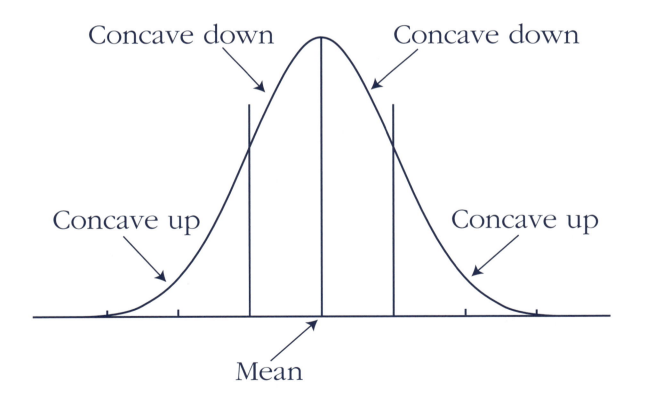

Concave down   Concave down

Concave up   Concave up

Mean

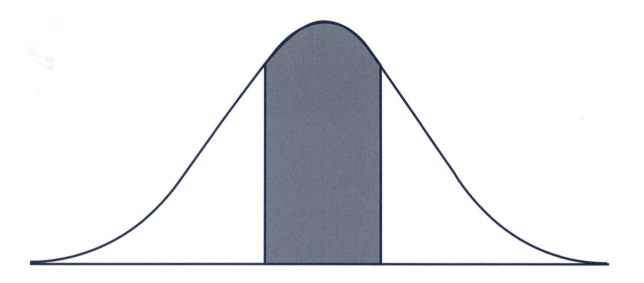

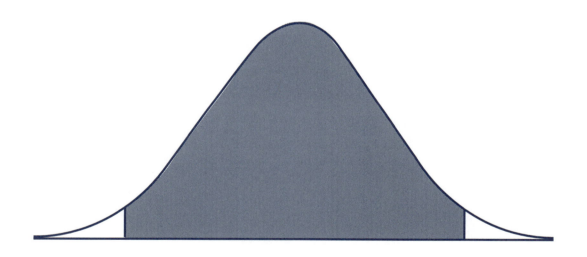

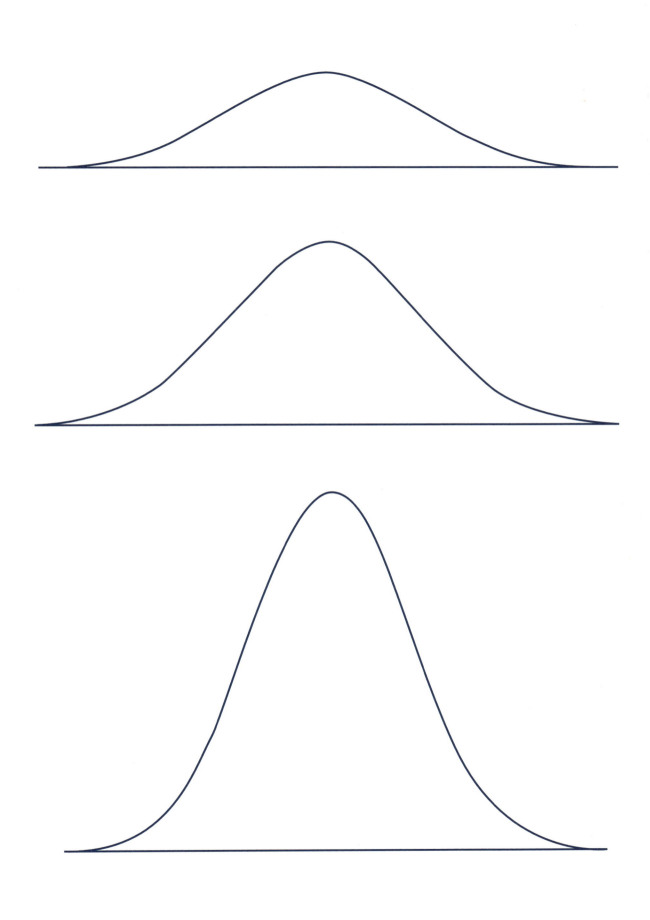

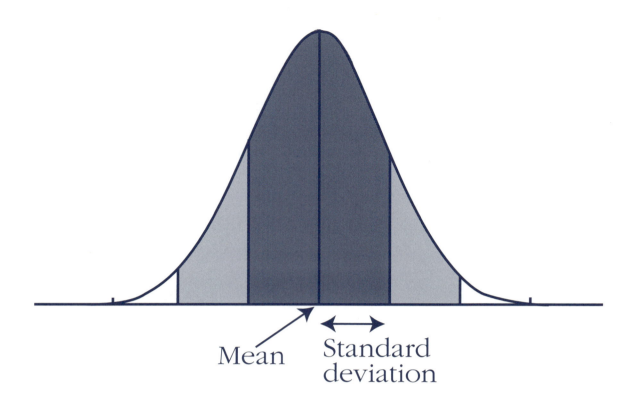

Mean   Standard
        deviation

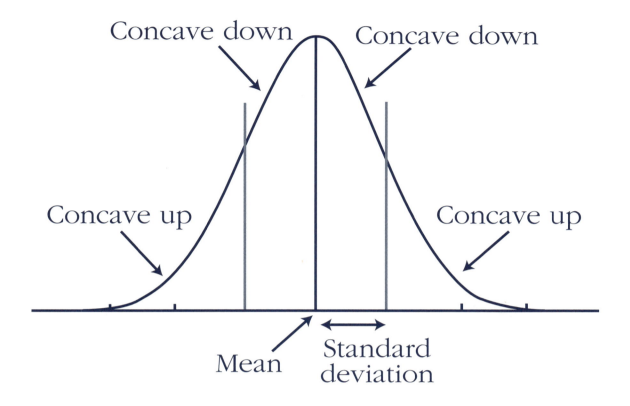

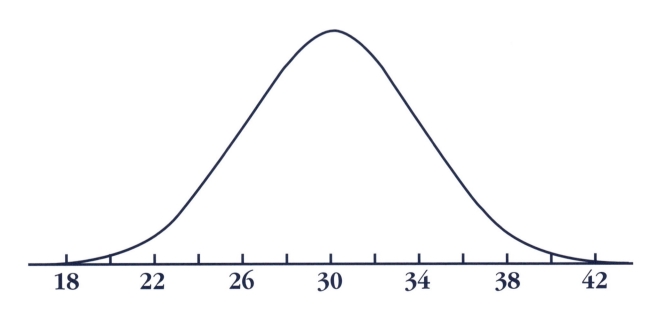

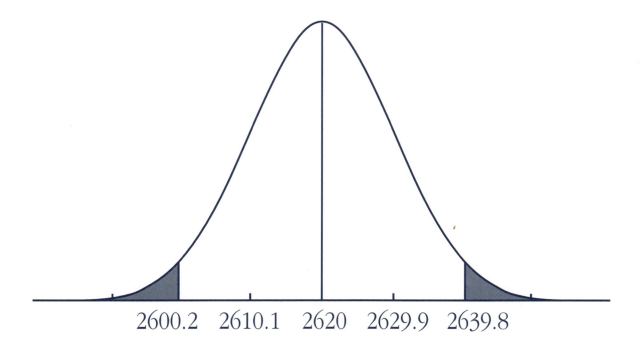

2600.2   2610.1   2620   2629.9   2639.8

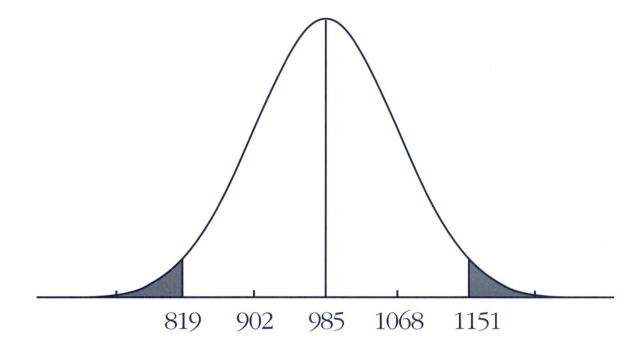

819 902 985 1068 1151

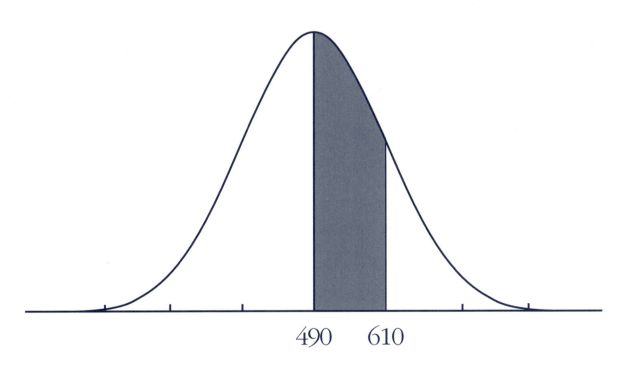

490 610

In-Class Assessment for "The Pit and the Pendulum"

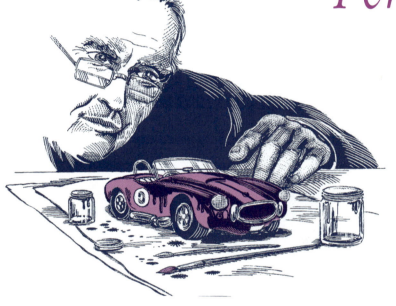

Steve works in a hobby shop. He was looking at the relationship between the length of certain models and the amount of paint they require.

Here are some estimates he came up with:

Length of Model (in feet)	Amount of Paint (in ounces)
1	2
2	6
3	14
5	40

Assuming that this pattern continues, estimate how much paint would be needed for a model that is 10 feet long. Explain your reasoning.

Take-Home Assessment for *The Pit and the Pendulum*

A circus performer wants to ride a bicycle right up to a brick wall and stop dramatically very close to the wall without crashing.

She wants to know when to apply the brakes.

She doesn't want to try the experiment because she is afraid of crashing. She just wants to predict at what point she should hit the brakes. However, she also realizes that no matter how hard she tries to make the conditions the same every time, there may be some variation in the distance required to stop her bicycle.

Devise a plan to collect and analyze data that will allow her to make this prediction, and describe how she might use the data.

Use the ideas of the unit, discussing the variables to consider, the problems she will encounter, normal distribution, and standard deviation.

Glossary

This is the glossary for all five units of IMP Year 1.

Absolute value The distance a number is from 0 on the number line. The symbol | | stands for absolute value.

Examples: $|-2| = 2$; $|7| = 7$; $|0| = 0$

Acute angle An angle that measures more than 0° and less than 90°.

Acute triangle A triangle whose angles are all acute.

Adjacent angles Two angles with the same vertex and formed using a shared ray.

Example: Angles A and B are adjacent angles.

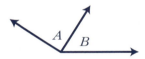

Adjacent side (for an acute angle of a right triangle) The side of the right triangle which, together with the hypotenuse, forms the given angle.

Example: In the right triangle ABC, side $\overline{BC}$ is adjacent to $\angle C$, and side $\overline{AB}$ is adjacent to $\angle A$.

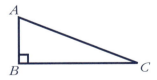

Alternate interior angles If two lines are intersected by a transversal, then the inside angles that are on opposite sides of the transversal are alternate interior angles.

Example: Angles *K* and *L* are one pair of alternate interior angles, and angles *M* and *N* are another pair.

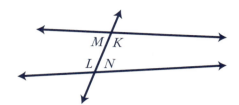

Amplitude   (for a pendulum) The angle of a pendulum's swing, measured from the vertical to the most outward position of the pendulum during its swing.

Example: The pendulum in the diagram has an amplitude of 20°.

Angle   Informally, an amount of turn, usually measured in **degrees.** Formally, the geometric figure formed by two **rays** with a common initial point, called the **vertex** of the angle.

Angle of elevation   The angle at which an object appears above the horizontal, as measured from a chosen point.

Example: The diagram shows the angle of elevation to the top of the tree from point *A*.

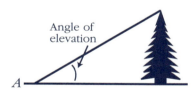

Area   Informally, the amount of space inside a two-dimensional figure, usually measured in square units.

Area model   For probability, a diagram showing the possible outcomes of a particular event. Each portion of the model represents an outcome, and the ratio of the area of that portion to the area of the whole model is the probability of that outcome.

Axis	(plural: **axes**) See **Coordinate system.**
Coefficient	Usually, a number being used to multiply a variable or power of a variable in an algebraic expression. Example: In the expression $3x + 4x^2$, 3 and 4 are coefficients.
Complementary angles	A pair of angles whose measures add to 90°. If two complementary angles are adjacent, together they form a right angle.
Composite number	A counting number having more than two whole-number divisors. Example: 12 is a composite number because it has the divisors 1, 2, 3, 4, 6, and 12.
Conclusion	Informally, any statement arrived at by reasoning or through examples. See also **"If . . . , then . . ." statement.**
Conditional probability	The probability that an event will occur based on the assumption that some other event has already occurred.
Congruent	Informally, having the same shape and size. Formally, two polygons are congruent if their corresponding angles have equal measure and their corresponding sides are equal in length. The symbol ≅ means "is congruent to."
Conjecture	A theory or an idea about how something works, usually based on examples.
Constraint	Informally, a limitation or restriction.
Continuous graph	Informally, a graph that can be drawn without lifting the pencil, in contrast to a **discrete graph.**
Coordinate system	A way to represent points in the plane with pairs of numbers called **coordinates.** The system is based on

two perpendicular lines, one horizontal and one vertical, called **coordinate axes.** The point where the lines meet is called the **origin.** Traditionally, the axes are labeled with the variables *x* and *y* as shown below. The horizontal axis is often called the ***x*-axis** and the vertical axis is often called the ***y*-axis.**

Example: Point *A* has coordinates (3, –2).

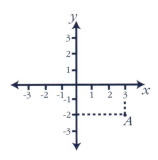

Corresponding angles

(for a transversal) If two lines are intersected by a transversal, then two angles are corresponding angles if they occupy the same position relative to the transversal and the other lines that form them.

Example: Angles *A* and *D* are a pair of corresponding angles, and angles *B* and *E* are another pair of corresponding angles.

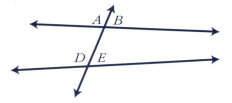

Corresponding parts

For a pair of similar or congruent polygons, sides or angles of the two polygons that have the same relative position.

Example: Side *a* in the small triangle and side *b* in the large triangle are corresponding parts.

 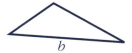

Counterexample   An example which demonstrates that a conjecture is not true.

Degree   The measurement unit for an angle defined by having a complete turn equal to 360 degrees. The symbol ° represents degrees.

Diagonal   In a polygon, a line segment that connects two vertices and that is not a side of the polygon.

Discrete graph   A graph consisting of isolated or unconnected points, in contrast to a **continuous graph.**

Divisor   A factor of an integer.

Example: 1, 2, 3, 4, 6, and 12 are the positive divisors of 12.

Domain   The set of values that can be used as inputs for a given function.

Equilateral triangle   A triangle with all sides the same length.

Expected value   In a game or other probability situation, the average amount gained or lost per turn in the long run.

Exterior angle   An angle formed outside a polygon by extending one of its sides.

Example: The diagram shows an exterior angle for polygon *ABCDE*.

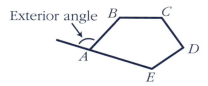

Factor   The same as **divisor.**

Factorial   The product of all the whole numbers from a particular number down to 1. The symbol ! stands for factorial.

Example: 5! (read "five factorial") means 5 · 4 · 3 · 2 · 1.

Fair game   A game in which both players are expected to come out equally well in the long run.

Frequency bar graph	A bar graph showing how often each result occurs.

Example: This frequency bar graph shows, for instance, that 11 times in 80 rolls, the sum of two dice was 6.

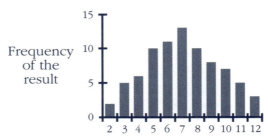

Function	Informally, a process or rule for determining the numerical value of one variable in terms of another. A function is often represented as a set of number pairs in which the second number is determined by the first, according to the function rule.
Graph	A mathematical diagram for displaying information.
Hexagon	A polygon with six sides.
Hypotenuse	The longest side in a right triangle, or the length of this side. The hypotenuse is located opposite the right angle.

Example: In right triangle *ABC*, the hypotenuse is $\overline{AC}$.

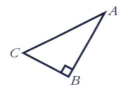

Hypothesis	Informally, a theory about a situation or about how a certain set of data is behaving. Also, a set of assumptions being used to analyze or understand a situation.

See also **"If . . . , then . . ." statement.**

"If . . . , then . . ." statement	A specific form of mathematical statement, saying that if one condition is true, then another condition must also be true.

Example: Here is a true "If . . . , then . . ." statement.

If two angles of a triangle have equal measure, then the sides opposite these angles have equal length.

The condition "two angles of a triangle have equal measure" is the **hypothesis.** The condition "the sides opposite these angles have equal length" is the **conclusion.**

Independent events	Two (or more) events are independent if the outcome of one does not influence the outcome of the other.

Integer

Any number that is either a counting number, zero, or the opposite of a counting number. The integers can be represented using set notation as

$$\{ \ldots -3, -2, -1, 0, 1, 2, 3, \ldots \}$$

Examples: $-4, 0$, and 10 are integers.

Interior angle

An angle inside a figure, especially within a polygon.

Example: Angle *BAE* is an interior angle of the polygon *ABCDE*.

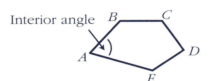

Isosceles triangle

A triangle with two sides of equal length.

Leg

Either of the two shorter sides in a right triangle. The two legs of a right triangle form the right angle of the triangle. The longest side of a right triangle (the hypotenuse) is not considered a leg.

Line of best fit

Informally, the line that comes closest to fitting a given set of points on a discrete graph.

Line segment

The portion of a straight line between two given points.

Mathematical model

A mathematical description or structure used to represent how a real-life situation works.

Mean

The numerical average of a data set, found by adding the data items and dividing by the number of items in the set.

Example: For the data set 8, 12, 12, 13, and 17, the sum of the data items is 62 and there are 5 items in the data set, so the mean is 62 ÷ 5, or 12.4.

Measurement variation

The situation of taking several measurements of the same thing and getting different results.

Median

(of a set of data) The "middle number" in a set of data that has been arranged from smallest to largest.

Example: For the data set 4, 17, 22, 56, and 100, the median is 22, because it is the number in the middle of the list.

Mode

(of a set of data) The number that occurs most often in a set of data. Many sets of data do not have a single mode.

Example: For the data set 3, 4, 7, 16, 18, 18, and 23, the mode is 18.

Natural number Any of the counting numbers 1, 2, 3, 4, and so on.

Normal distribution

A certain precisely defined set of probabilities, which can often be used to approximate real-life events. Sometimes used to refer to any data set whose frequency bar graph is approximately "bell-shaped."

Observed probability

The likelihood of a certain event happening based on observed results, as distinct from **theoretical probability.**

Obtuse angle

An angle that measures more than 90° and less than 180°.

Obtuse triangle   A triangle with an obtuse angle.

Octagon   An eight-sided polygon.

Opposite side   The side of a triangle across from a given angle.

Order of operations

A set of conventions that mathematicians have agreed to use whenever a calculation involves more than one operation.

Example: 2 + 3 · 4 is 14, not 20, because the conventions for order of operations tell us to multiply before we add.

Ordered pair   Two numbers paired together using the format *(x, y)*, often used to locate a point in the coordinate system.

Origin   See **Coordinate system.**

Parallel lines   Two lines in a plane that do not intersect.

Pentagon   A five-sided polygon.

Perimeter   The boundary of a polygon, or the total length of this boundary.

Period   The length of time for a cyclical event to complete one full cycle.

Perpendicular lines   A pair of lines that form a right angle.

Polygon   A closed two-dimensional shape formed by three or more line segments. The line segments that form a polygon are called its sides. The endpoints of these segments are called **vertices** (singular: **vertex**).

Examples: All the figures below are polygons.

Prime number   A whole number greater than 1 that has only two whole number divisors, 1 and itself.

Example: 7 is a prime number, because its only whole number divisors are 1 and 7.

Probability   The likelihood of a certain event happening. For a situation involving equally likely outcomes, the probability that the outcome of an event will be an outcome within a given set is defined by a ratio:

$$\text{Probability} = \frac{\text{number of outcomes in the set}}{\text{total number of possible outcomes}}$$

Example: If a die has 2 red faces and 4 green faces, the probability of getting a green face is

$$\frac{\text{number of green faces}}{\text{total number of faces}} = \frac{4}{6}$$

Proof   An absolutely convincing argument.

Proportion   A statement that two ratios are equal.

Proportional   Having the same ratio.

Example: Corresponding sides of triangles *ABC* and *DEF* are proportional, because the ratios $\frac{4}{6}$, $\frac{8}{12}$, and $\frac{10}{15}$ are equal.

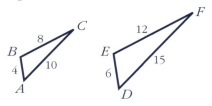

Quadrant   One of the four areas created in a coordinate system by using the *x*-axis and the *y*-axis as boundaries. The quadrants have standard numbering as shown below.

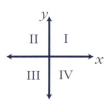

Quadrilateral   A four-sided polygon.

Random   Used in probability to indicate that any of several events is equally likely or that an event is selected from a set of events according to a precisely described distribution.

Range   (of a set of data) The difference between the largest and smallest numbers in the set.

Example: For the data set 7, 12, 18, 18, and 29, the range is 29 – 7, or 22.

Ray   The part of a line from a single point, called the **vertex,** through another point on the line and continuing infinitely in that direction.

Rectangle	A four-sided polygon whose angles are all right angles.
Regular polygon	A polygon whose sides all have equal length and whose angles all have equal measure.
Rhombus	A four-sided polygon whose sides all have the same length.
Right angle	An angle that measures 90°.
Right triangle	A triangle with a right angle.
Sample standard deviation	The calculation on a set of data taken from a larger population of data, used to estimate the standard deviation of the larger population.
Sequence	A list of numbers or expressions, usually following a pattern or rule.
	Example: 1, 3, 5, 7, 9, . . . is the sequence of positive odd numbers.
Similar	Informally, having the same shape. Formally, two polygons are similar if their corresponding angles have equal measure and their corresponding sides are proportional in length. The symbol ~ means "is similar to."
Simulation	An experiment or set of experiments using a model of a certain event that is based on the same probabilities as the real event. Simulations allow people to estimate the likelihood of an event when it is impractical to experiment with the real event.
Slope	Informally, the steepness of a line.
Solution	A number that, when substituted for a variable in an equation, makes the equation a true statement.
	Example: The value $x = 3$ is a solution to the equation $2x = 6$ because $2 \cdot 3 = 6$.
Square	A four-sided polygon with all sides of equal length and with four right angles.

Square root	A number whose square is a given number. The symbol $\sqrt{}$ is used to denote the nonnegative square root of a number. Example: Both 6 and –6 are square roots of 36, because $6^2 = 36$ and $(-6)^2 = 36$; $\sqrt{36} = 6$.
Standard deviation	A specific measurement of how spread out a set of data is, usually represented by the lowercase Greek letter sigma (σ).
Straight angle	An angle that measures 180°. The rays forming a straight angle together make up a straight line.
Strategy	A complete plan about how to proceed in a game or problem situation. A strategy for a game should tell a person exactly what to do under any situation that can arise in the game.
Supplementary angles	A pair of angles whose measures add to 180°. If two supplementary angles are adjacent, together they form a straight angle.
Term	(of an algebraic expression) A part of an algebraic expression, combined with other terms using addition or subtraction. Example: The expression $2x^2 + 3x - 12$ has three terms: $2x^2$, $3x$, and 12.
Term	(of a sequence) One of the items listed in a sequence. Example: In the sequence 3, 5, 7, . . . , the number 3 is the first term, 5 is the second term, and so on.
Theoretical probability	The likelihood of an event occurring, as explained by a theory or model, as distinct from **observed probability.**
Transversal	A line that intersects two or more other lines.

Example: The line *l* is a transversal that intersects the lines *m* and *n*.

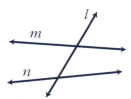

Trapezoid

A four-sided polygon with exactly one pair of parallel sides.

Example: Quadrilateral *PQRS* is a trapezoid, because $\overline{QR}$ and $\overline{PS}$ are parallel and $\overline{PQ}$ and $\overline{SR}$ are not parallel.

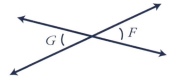

Triangle

A polygon with three sides.

Triangle inequality principle

The principle that the lengths of any two sides of a triangle must add up to more than the length of the third side.

Trigonometric function

Any of six functions defined for acute angles in terms of ratios of sides of a right triangle.

Vertex

(plural: **vertices**) See **Angle, Polygon,** and **Ray.**

Vertical angles

A pair of "opposite" angles formed by a pair of intersecting lines.

Example: Angles *F* and *G* are vertical angles.

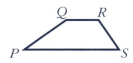

Whole number

A number that is either zero or a counting number.

x-intercept

A place on a graph where a line or curve crosses the *x*-axis.

y-intercept

A place on a graph where a line or curve crosses the *y*-axis.

Photographic Credits

Teacher Book Classroom Photography

4 Tamalpais High School, Sherry Fraser; **23** Santa Cruz High School, Lynne Alper; **33** Roosevelt High School, Lynn Alper; **38** Clovis High School, Lynne Alper; **44** Lincoln High School, Lori Green **54** Santa Cruz High School, Lynne Alper, **78** Napa High School, Lynne Alper, **92** Foothill High School, Cheryl Dozier, **168** Clovis High School, Lynne Alper, **175** Fresno High School, Lynne Alper

Student Book Classroom Photography

3 Lincoln High School, Lori Green; **14** Lincoln High School, Lori Green; **27** Lincoln High School, Lori Green; **36** Lincoln High School, Lori Green; **42** San Lorenzo Valley High School, Kim Gough; **55** Lincoln High School, Lori Green; **95** Foothill High School, Sheryl Dozier; **104** Foothill High School, Sheryl Dozier; **114** Mendocino Community High School, Lynne Alper; **127** Mendocino High School, Lynne Alper; **150** Lake View High School, Carol Caref; **157** West High School, Janice Bussey; **189** Whitney Young High School, Carol Berland; **210** Pleasant Valley High School, Michael Christensen; **222** Lynne Alper; **238** East Bakersfield High School, Susan Lloyd; **252** Lincoln High School, Lynne Alper; **274** Colton High School, Sharon Taylor; **281** Foothill High School, Sheryl Dozier; **307** Santa Cruz High School, Lynne Alper; **324** Foothill High School, Cheryl Dozier; **352** Santa Maria High School, Mike Bryant; **366** Santa Cruz High School, Lynne Alper; **373** Shasta High School, Dave Robathan; **397** Santa Cruz High School, Lynne Alper; **414** Santa Maria High School, Mike Bryant; **424** Bartram Communications Academy, Robert Powlen; **446** Santa Maria High School, Mike Bryant; **460** Ranum High School, Rita Quintana

Front Cover Students

Katrina Van Loan, Jenee Desmond, David Trammell, Gina Uriarte, Thea Singleton, Itan Novis, Sarah N. Weintraub (photographed by Hilary Turner at Tamalpais High School)